CON\ with GOD in ADVENT and CHRISTMAS

PRAYING THE SUNDAY MASS READINGS

WITH *LECTIO DIVINA*

CONVERSING *with* GOD *in* ADVENT *and* CHRISTMAS

PRAYING THE SUNDAY MASS READINGS WITH *LECTIO DIVINA*

STEPHEN J. BINZ

Published by The Word Among Us Press
7115 Guilford Road
Frederick, Maryland 21704
www.wau.org

16 15 14 13 12   1 2 3 4 5

ISBN: 978-1-59325-208-3
e-ISBN: 978-1-59325-438-4

Cover design by Faceout Studios

Made and printed in the United States of America.

Library of Congress Cataloging-in-Publication Data

Binz, Stephen J., 1955-
  Conversing with God in Advent and Christmas : praying the Sunday Mass
readings with lectio divina / Stephen J. Binz.
       p. cm.
  ISBN 978-1-59325-208-3
  1. Advent—Prayers and devotions. 2. Christmas—Prayers and devotions.
3. Catholic Church--Prayers and devotions. 4. Bible--Devotional literature.
5. Catholic Church. Lectionary for Mass (U.S.) I. Title.
  BX2170.A4B535 2012
  242'.33--dc23
                              2012024428

Dedicated to
my wife, Pamela,

whose favorite color is purple,
and whose favorite sight is the soft glow of candles.
She is the one with whom I hope to spend
every Advent and Christmas.

Contents

Preface

The practice of lectio divina continues to grow, not only in its seedbed within the Catholic and Orthodox traditions, but in Protestant and Evangelical communities as well. Christians everywhere are rediscovering the rich potential of this ancient practice. This contemplative and transforming response to Sacred Scripture is bringing about, as Pope Benedict XVI predicted, a "new springtime" in the Church. The teachings of bishops and spiritual masters have encouraged the practice of lectio divina for all the people of God.

In my first book in this series, *Conversing with God in Scripture: A Contemporary Approach to Lectio Divina*, I pondered this spiritual tradition and explored ways in which this ancient art could be cultivated by people in our day. I reflected on the movements—lectio, meditatio, oratio, contemplatio, and operatio—and suggested ways that readers might incorporate lectio divina into their lives as disciples. I concluded with a few examples of how selected passages of Scripture could be taken up in lectio divina and lead the reader to interior transformation.

A favorable response to this first book prompted The Word Among Us Press to ask me to continue this approach to lectio divina with the Lectionary readings of the liturgical cycle. What follows is a consideration of the tradition of lectio divina during Advent and Christmas and an exposition of the Sunday readings of the Lectionary based in the five established movements of the practice.

As in the previous book, I have created a work that can be used either privately or in groups. Individuals may use it for their own reflective practice, or churches and communities may wish to incorporate it into their Advent and Christmas journey together. It is ideal for liturgical ministers, catechists, RCIA teams, catechumens and candidates, those involved in adult faith formation, and all in the parish who are engaged in spiritual growth.

How to Use This Book

If you choose to use this book for your own personal growth, simply spend some quiet time during each week of the Advent and Christmas seasons with the Scripture readings of the upcoming Sunday. As in my previous book, *Conversing with God in Lent*, I have selected the first reading and the Gospel, as these readings are designed to relate to and complement one another. The five movements of lectio divina will guide you through the reflective process. Led by the Holy Spirit, you can expect to be changed and renewed by God's living word through this ancient practice. Realize that this book is only a guide—you should feel free to follow as many or as few of the suggestions as you choose. For example, don't think that you must meditate on each of the questions provided. You will be led to reflect on whatever the Holy Spirit brings to your mind and heart after each Scripture passage.

If you choose to follow this book with a small group, you will reap the wisdom and support of others, which can be an enormous help in experiencing the transforming power of Scripture (see the chapter "*Collatio*: Forming Community through Scripture" in *Conversing with God in Scripture*). Groups should meet once a week during this liturgical season to reflect together on the

Scriptures for the upcoming Sunday, or they may meet immediately after the Mass to continue the prayerful listening to that Sunday's readings. Members should read the first two chapters of this book in advance and, if they wish, may reflect on the questions of the meditatio at home before coming to the group session. A facilitator guides the group through each step of lectio divina, honoring each movement with the attention it requires. Most of the discussion will center on the questions of the meditatio, but the group should feel free to decide which questions to consider and should not be compelled to discuss them all.

Prepare the Way

If you often feel like your December calendar is more of a frenzied list of details to accomplish rather than an Advent calendar of holy anticipation, you might consider taking up the practice of lectio divina during these days. If the pre-Christmas rush is not balanced by the sacred waiting of Advent, you may find yourself physically and emotionally exhausted and spiritually empty by the time Christmas arrives. Make time to pray and listen to God in his word. As he changes your heart, you will experience the peaceful joy of the Incarnation.

Stephen J. Binz

Chapter 1

Prayerfully Listening to God's Word during Advent and Christmas

The spirit of Advent and Christmas can best be cultivated by practicing the ancient art of lectio divina. These special seasons are all about expectation—waiting for and anticipating the coming of Jesus Christ. This is also the purpose of lectio divina. We listen carefully to Scripture with expectation, confident that God is going to do something new in our lives through our encounter with his word. Through our prayerful listening to the sacred text, we expect to meet Christ there. We trust that the same Holy Spirit who inspired the Scriptures will also move in our hearts to transform us and create us anew.

The goal of our practices during Advent is to deepen our longing for Jesus, for his coming into our hearts and for his glorious coming at the end of time. We prepare to celebrate the great mystery of the Incarnation that is at the heart of Christian faith. This interior longing is the source of all prayer, and lectio divina cultivates that deep desire for Christ.

During Advent we hear the stories of our ancestors as they longed for the coming of the Messiah. These stories teach us to be receptive and to open our hearts to God's initiative. Christmas teaches us to receive God's gifts with joy and gratitude, to realize, like Mary, that "the Mighty One has done great things for me" (Luke 1:49). This receptivity to God's grace is cultivated by the practice of lectio divina. We learn to approach Scripture with a receptive and expectant spirit. We open our hearts to God's initiative and listen carefully for the gifts God offers us in his word. We realize that our lives are a response to the love that God has first shown us in Christ. We respond to God in prayer, not so much to do something for God, but more important, to open our hearts to God's greatest gift—the coming of his Son, Jesus Christ, to us.

The Coming of the Lord

The Bible ends with the words of Christ, "Yes, I am coming soon," and with the ancient prayer of the Church, "Come, Lord Jesus!" (Revelation 22:20). The word "Advent" is derived from the Latin word *adventus,* which means "coming." In Advent we're reminded of how much we need a savior, and we look forward to our Savior's coming in majesty even as we prepare to remember his coming in humility at Bethlehem.

Like our ancestors in Israel who longed for the Messiah, and like the early Christians who longed for the return of Christ in glory, we heighten our yearning during this season. The future that this season urges us to focus on is the new creation, the new Jerusalem, the kingdom of God in its fullness. In that coming future, war will be a thing of the past, and there will be no more hunger, sickness, poverty, or death. No one will ever be abused or exploited again, and all of God's creation will live in love and in peace. Our Savior wants us to spend time every day during Advent remembering his promise that he will come again so that we can find the right balance between living in the present and longing for the age to come.

But the purpose of our looking to the future and remembering the past is to deepen the quality of our living in the present. As the gospels tell us, both John the Baptist and Jesus proclaimed, "The kingdom of God is at hand!" (Mark 1:15; cf. Matthew 4:17). When we wait with expectant hope for the coming of the Lord in glory and remember with grateful joy the coming of Jesus incarnate in our world, we realize more intensely the sacredness of the present. In every moment we are coming to a richer and fuller future when Christ will make all things new. But also at every moment, as we place our hope in Christ and live in joyful anticipation, Jesus is coming to us. We will experience the blessings of God's kingdom to the extent that we live fully engaged in the present, working for justice and peace, reaching out to those most in need of our love and care. The coming of Christ is not just in the past or in the undetermined future; it is right here today. He is continually being born in our midst and transforming his Church ever more into his body in the world.

The Season of Lighting the Darkness

In the late autumn of the year, as the days become short and the world grows dim, the peoples of the earth lighten the darkness. In ancient times, participants in the pagan Yule celebrations lit oil lamps in the darkness. Our spiritual ancestors in Judaism burned lamps during their Festival of Dedication and today light the candles of the Hanukkah menorah as an expression of gratitude for God's saving presence. Christians light the candles of the Advent wreath as a symbol of increasing expectation. People of many religious persuasions light their homes and their cities during this season. The light of December is not flashing or blinding; it is the glow of lamps and candles that brighten the darkness, the light that comes before the rising dawn.

Both Jews and Christians look forward with joyful hope for the Messiah's future coming. These two heirs of Israel's ancient faith listen to the prophets to understand the dawning light that God will bring in our future. Of course, the Jewish people hope for the Messiah's first manifestation while Christians await his return. But we can be sure that Jews and Christians look forward together to the future appearance of God's same Anointed One. The whole world awaits a time of peace and justice in the world; all people dream of a future in which all creation is whole and complete. And we know that the God of all creation and of all the nations is the source of that trusting optimism. During Advent we wait in our dark world, united with all the expectant people of the earth in mutual hope for the future's rising dawn.

For some people, this holiday season is a time of delight, time off from school and work for happy gatherings of family and friends, for giving and receiving gifts. For others, it is a dreaded time as they approach the holiday with memories of those with whom they can no longer celebrate or with worry about how they will pay for the gifts and meals they want to provide. For the friendless, the homeless, the imprisoned, and the abused, the season may arouse bitter regrets or painful comparisons. In life's gloominess, candles proclaim that light has more right to exist than darkness. The increasing light of the Advent wreath and the gleaming lights of Christmas remind us that as followers of the Light of the world, we must catch fire from the light of Christ's mystery and bring something of this fire and light into our own lives and into the lives of those who walk in darkness.

Christ is our light. Whatever our situation, the Scripture readings of this season help us to adopt a stance of faithful waiting. In quiet stillness, we attune our hearts to watch for him. Truly our hope is in the Lord. In silence we ponder the great mystery of our salvation. As Christians living in the midst of our secular and consumer society, we observe this season as a countersign to the shallow pleasures offered to us by the world. We must take care that our busyness does not distract us lest we be caught unaware and unprepared for what God wishes to do within us and among us.

For most of Christian history, before the age of the printing press and electric lighting, people read the sacred text of Scripture with the light of oil lamps. The handwritten pages were often a word of art, offering doorways into the mysteries that the text revealed. The luminous manuscripts spotlighted the treasure of God's word contained within. Even today our printed Bibles can express to us the mystery of Christ that lies inside the *sacra pagina*. The words and images that emerge from the texts of this season offer entryways leading to the one who comes in the midst of darkness to be with us. The enlightening Spirit who dwells within these inspired words and who has illuminated the minds and hearts of our ancestors before us also moves within us to lead us to Christ.

The Great Prophetic Figures of Advent and Christmas

All the great prophets of Israel's Scriptures were important for preparing God's people for the Messiah's coming, but Isaiah soars above the rest. As a poet, he uses vivid and powerful images to convey his message, and his writings have an extraordinary literary quality. He warns God's people to repent, comforts them with assurances of God's faithful promises, and offers hope for a messianic king who will come to save and usher in a new age when all creation will see God's glory.

In the three-year Lectionary cycle, Isaiah's voice rings out over all the others as the first reading during Advent and Christmas time. Of the twelve Advent Sundays, Isaiah is proclaimed seven times—on all four Sundays in Year A and the first three Sundays in Year B. In Year C the first readings are taken from four different Old Testament prophets: Jeremiah, Baruch, Zephaniah, and Micah. Isaiah's message is also proclaimed as the first reading on Christmas, Epiphany, and the Baptism of the Lord.

Guiding our way through Advent as we prepare for Christmas, Isaiah invites us to look forward to the coming of the Messiah and to prepare the way of the Lord. He urges us to tear down the mountains of our misdeeds and fill in the valleys of our injustices and to make the way straight for our God. Isaiah urges us to obey the Lord's instruction, walk in the ways of peace, follow the promptings of the Spirit, and be just in thought, word, and deed.

Eight centuries before the time of Jesus, Isaiah anticipated the coming of the ideal king. The young maiden will bear a son and name him Immanuel, a name that means "with us is God." The child will be called Wonder-Counselor, Prince of Peace, and his dominion will be vast and forever peaceful. This sprouting shoot from the stump of Jesse will judge the poor with justice and decide fairly for those who are afflicted. The spirit of the Lord shall rest upon him, and he will decisively change the course of human history.

Isaiah's prophecies extend into the season of Christmas because he spoke so hopefully of the coming of God's kingdom. Voicing words of hope to God's people during their exile, Isaiah offered new possibilities and new beginnings. He offered comfort when times seemed most discouraging and the image of dawning light in the darkest of times. He was the first to clearly articulate that the God of Israel was also the God of all people. God's saving mercy would reach beyond the boundaries of Jerusalem and Judah to extend to all peoples in every corner of the earth.

The other great prophetic figure of this season is John the Baptist. He is the last of a long line of prophets preparing God's people for the Messiah's coming. But he didn't prepare with a sweet sentimentality about a smiling baby born on a starry night. His distinctive voice is clear and bold, calling the people to repentance. He makes the prophetic voice of Isaiah the mission of his life: "Prepare the way of the Lord, make straight his paths" (Mark 1:3). He proclaims the message that those anticipating the Messiah must renew their lives to get ready. "Repent," he says, for "the kingdom of God is at hand" (Mark 1:15; cf. Matthew 3:2).

John the Baptist went out into the desert of Judea to listen. The Hebrew word for desert is *midvar*, and its root is the word *davar*, meaning "word" or "message." The desert is that place where God's word can be heard without interruption, freed from all the distractions that could prevent the hearer from responding to and living that divine word. Religious leaders and visionaries have often gone to the desert to listen intently for God's voice and discover new ways to live. John was a credible preacher of repentance because he first came to love God's word, which he heard in the midst of his own desert. During this season, we, too, can carve out a little desert in the midst of our activities. We can go to that quiet place and allow God's word to speak to us, reorient us, and lead us to Christ who is always coming toward us.

John concludes the Old Testament messianic longing and initiates the New Testament recognition of the Messiah. His image is often portrayed with his finger pointing to the one who was coming: Jesus Christ. He helps us prepare our lives so that we will recognize the Messiah and give him an appropriate welcome. The real preparation to which he calls us is repentance, which includes a change of heart and a transformation of our lives. This Advent prophet tells us that our task is urgent. "Produce good fruit as evidence of your repentance," he proclaims (Matthew 3:8), knowing that conversion of our hearts must be evident in the way we live.

Both Isaiah and John the Baptist teach us that there is a way out of the darkness and sadness of the world and of the human condition, and that way is Jesus himself. The Messiah comes to save us from the powers of darkness and death and put us back on the path of peace and reconciliation so that we might find our way back to God. We should heed that call of the prophets and make this season a time of real change so that our royal Savior will be welcomed into our lives.

The Blessed Virgin Mary in Advent and Christmas

Our best model for lectio divina during this season is Mary of Nazareth. Many images of the Annunciation depict Mary as reading from the Hebrew Scriptures when the angel appears to her. The meaning of such imagery is that Mary was a woman steeped in the tradition of ancient Israel. She knew the prophets and psalms and reflected on them daily in her heart. Mary was immersed in the word before the Word became "immersed" in her.

Luke's Gospel says that Mary "kept all these things in her heart," reflecting on them (2:51). What did Mary treasure and ponder in her heart? It was the words of the ancient Scriptures that she had learned throughout her life, the new message the angel had revealed to her, the words the shepherds had said about her child, and the words that welled up within her as she sang her canticle of praise. By reflecting on these things, making connections between the ancient and the new, between what God had done for her people Israel and was now doing in her own life, Mary grew in understanding of God's plan and responded to God's will with her continual acceptance.

After Gabriel announces to Mary that she is favored by God and is to bear a son, all creation awaits her response. The advent of Christ hangs on her willingness to accept the angelic message. God asks Mary to give her whole self over to his saving plan. Her acceptance, "May it be done to me according to your word" (Luke 1:38), was in large part due to her daily discipline of listening to God's word in Scripture and reflecting on that word with watchfulness, prayerfulness, and expectation.

This Gospel portrayal of Mary challenges us. To what words and images do we give our attention? How do we keep in tune with God's voice and remain responsive to his plan? Our task during the Advent and Christmas seasons is to imitate Mary by meditating on the word of God and allowing it to resonate within our hearts and pour out into our lives. The Sunday Scriptures of the Church's Lectionary will bring us into the presence of that word and help us to wait in joyful hope. Israel's prophets, John the Baptist, Joseph, Mary, the angels, the shepherds, and the Magi all experienced expectation and wonder as they realized that God was doing new things in the world and in their individual lives. May we, too, feel that same expectation and wonder as we see God's work unfolding in our lives.

Chapter Two

Lectio Divina for All God's People

Lectio divina is the Church's most ancient way of studying Scripture. Rooted in the Jewish tradition, the art of lectio divina has been nurtured through the desert spirituality of the early centuries, the patristic writers of the ancient Church, and the monastic tradition through the ages. In today's worldwide revival of this age-old wisdom, Christians are learning how to experience Scripture in a time-tested and deeper way by listening to and conversing with God through the inspired texts.

The only real purpose of lectio divina is to lead us to a personal encounter and dialogue with God. It is not a highly specialized method of prayer or a methodical system with required steps that must be rigidly followed.[1] The ancient spiritual masters always distrusted methods of prayer that were defined too severely. They knew that God's Spirit moves differently in each person and that God's inner work within the individual should not be impeded with unyielding rules. So there is no need to anxiously assess our spiritual practice as if we had to follow it "correctly" to achieve some particular target. There is no goal other than prayerfully reading Scripture in God's presence with a desire to deepen our heart-to-heart intimacy with him. In lectio divina we let go of our own agenda and gradually open

---

1. My previous work, *Conversing with God in Scripture: A Contemporary Approach to Lectio Divina*, explains how *The Monk's Ladder*, by the twelfth century Carthusian monk Guigo II, unintentionally calcified the practice of lectio divina for subsequent centuries in a way that was far more rigidly and hierarchically defined than in the earlier centuries.

ourselves to what God wants us to experience through the sacra pagina, the inspired text.

The five components of lectio divina, which are outlined here, are best described as "movements," as distinguished from hierarchical steps or rungs on a ladder. This terminology allows for a certain amount of spontaneous freedom within the prayerful practice, as was characteristic of the practice in the Church's early centuries.

Lectio: Reading the Text with a Listening Ear

We begin by setting aside the time and sanctifying the space for our reading. We might want to place a cross or an icon in front of us, light a candle, or offer some gesture to highlight the moment. Placing the Bible or Lectionary text in our hands, we first call on the Holy Spirit to guide our minds and hearts in the presence of God's word.

We read the text slowly and attentively. We try to set aside any preconceived ideas about what the text is going to say. We read reverently and expectantly, knowing that God is going to speak to us in some new way, offering us some new wisdom and understanding through the inspired text.

Though lectio is often translated as "reading," the tradition suggests much more than ordinary reading. It is more like listening deeply. In lectio God is teaching us to listen to his voice within the words on the page. It often helps to return to the ancient practice of reading texts of Scripture aloud. In this way we both see the text with our eyes and hear the words with our ears, encouraging a fuller comprehension and experience of the word.

Giving our whole attention to the words, we allow ourselves to enjoy the Scriptures. Savoring the words, images, metaphors, and characters, we grow to appreciate and love the text itself. Paying attention to its literary form, we realize that God's truth is expressed in a variety of ways through many types of literature in the Bible.

Biblical scholarship and commentary can help us understand more of the context of the passage by shedding light on what the authors meant to communicate in the text. The Jewish rabbinical tradition and the writings of Church Fathers in the early centuries show us how artificial it is to make a distinction between the study of a text and prayerful reading. Grappling with the text, searching for fuller understanding, can be a prayerful and faith-filled process. The work of scholars can help us probe all the potential the text can offer us.

STUDY c/b PRAYER

Finally, we must always ask how the writer's faith manifests itself in the text and what kind of faith response the writer wishes to elicit from us as readers. Emphasizing the faith dimension of a text helps us transcend the original circumstances in which it was written and allows us to see its lasting influence and universal validity.

② Meditatio: Reflecting on the Meaning and Message of the Text

PROBING SEEKING

The eyes and ears and even the mind are not the final destination of God's word. We listen to the sacred text so that the words of Scripture might finally inhabit our hearts. When we have created space in our hearts for the word to dwell, the sacred texts can make their home in us, residing in the deepest part of our beings so that they become a part of us.

We can begin to open our hearts to God's word as we establish connections between the text of ancient times and our lives today. Either a word or phrase in the text reminds us of something that has happened in our experience, or something that has happened reminds us of the text. In meditatio we ponder a text until it becomes like a mirror, reflecting some of our own experiences, challenges, thoughts, and questions.

When the patristic writers of the early Church interpreted the Bible, they considered their work satisfactory only when they had found a meaning in the text that was relevant to the situation of Christians in their own day. Because God is the author of Scripture, he can speak to the present through the scriptural record of the past. As the word of God, the Bible has a richness that can be discovered in every age and in every culture. It has a particular message that can be received by every reader who listens to God's word in the context of his or her daily experiences.

A helpful way to meditate on a scriptural passage is to ask questions of the text. Some questions will help us make the connections: What aspects of the biblical world resemble our situation today? What aspects of our present condition does the text seem to address? What is the text's message for us right now? Other questions help us focus on more personal aspects of the text that we might want to reflect on in a deeper way: What emotions and memories does this text evoke in me? Where do I hear Christ speaking to me most personally in these verses? What grace is this text offering me? Often we will notice that rather than us questioning the Scriptures, they are questioning us. The

Wow

text will challenge us to go beyond our current level of comfort and security: What attitudes or habits must I change in order to truly live these inspired words? Why am I so resistant to reflecting on this text more carefully? After reading a passage of the Bible, we shouldn't be surprised if it begins to read us.

The more we meditate on God's word, the more it seeps into our lives and saturates our thoughts and feelings. St. Ambrose, a fourth-century bishop and Doctor of the Church, described this assimilation: "When we drink from sacred Scripture, the life-sap of the eternal Word penetrates the veins of our soul and our inner faculties."[2] This is the purpose of meditatio. It allows the dynamic word of God to so penetrate our lives that it truly infuses our minds and hearts, and we begin to embody its truth and its love.

Oratio: Praying in Response to God's Word

Lectio divina is essentially a dialogue with God, a gentle oscillation between listening to God and responding to him in prayer. As lectio moves into meditatio and we listen in a way that becomes increasingly more personal, we recognize that God is speaking to us and offering us a message that is unique to our own lives. Once we realize God's call to us, his personal challenge to us, or the insight he is trying to give us, we must answer in some way. This is the moment for prayer.

Our response to God in oratio is not just any form of prayer. In the context of lectio divina, oratio is rooted directly in prayerful reading and meditation on the scriptural text. In oratio the words, images, and sentiments of the biblical text combine with the ideas,

---

2. Ambrose, *Commentaries on the Psalms* I, 33: *Patrologia Latina* 14, 984.

feelings, memories, and desires arising within us. The words of Scripture, then, enter into our prayer language. The style and vocabulary of our personal prayers are enriched by the inspired words of our long biblical tradition. Our prayers no longer consist of repeated formulas; they resonate with the faith, hope, and love that animated the people of the Bible in their journey with God.

So the biblical words that were at the center of our listening become the heart of our response as well. Our prayer becomes a healthy combination of God's word and the words God moves us to say. The rich deposit God leaves within us after we have meditated on his word nourishes our prayer so that it becomes a heartfelt and Spirit-led response to him. When our prayer does not arise from our listening and is separated from the biblical text, it can become excessively private, egotistical, or eccentric. But when our prayer remains close to the inspired page, we know that we are responding in a way that goes directly to the heart of God.

The tone of our prayer will depend on what we hear God saying to us in our lectio and meditatio. When the text reminds us of the goodness, truth, or beauty of God and his action in our lives, we pray in praise and thanksgiving. When it makes us aware of the wrong we have done or the good we have failed to do, we pray with repentance and seek forgiveness. When the text reminds us of our own needs or the needs of others, we pray in petition. In some cases, our prayer may even be a rebellion, a crying lament, or an angry tirade, as we see in the literature of Job, Jeremiah, and some of the psalms. The key to oratio is that our prayerful response to God flows directly from our listening.

The most essential element of oratio is desire. In fact, St. Augustine said, "The desire to pray is itself prayer."[3] Because we are made for God and only God satisfies our deepest longing, the greatest desire of the human heart is for God. Prayer happens at that moment when our desire for God meets God's desire for us. So when we pray, we are speaking with God who knows us intimately, cares about us deeply, and accepts us unconditionally. When we discover an ability and desire to pray within our hearts, we know that it is a gift of the Holy Spirit. In reality, our desire for God is itself the presence of the Spirit working within us.

Contemplatio: Quietly Resting in God

The movement into contemplatio is a progression from conversation with God to communion with God. After listening to the Scriptures, reflecting on them, and responding to God in the words of our prayer, we then enter into silence. Resting in the divine presence, we simply accept and receive the transforming embrace of God who has led us to this moment.

Both oratio and contemplatio are prayer that arises from the heart. Oratio is word-filled prayer in response to God's word to us. Contemplatio is prayer with few if any words. It is the response to God that remains after words are no longer necessary or helpful. It is simply enjoying the experience of quietly being in God's presence. We no longer have a need to think or reason, listen or speak.

Of all the movements of lectio divina, contemplatio is the most difficult to describe because it is such a personal moment with God. But it is an essential part of the practice and should never be

---

3. Augustine, *Explanations of the Psalms*, 37, 14: *Patrologia Latina* 36, 404.

passed over. In fact, one could argue that contemplatio is the most essential element of lectio divina, even though it seems the most "useless" from a practical point of view.

Moving into contemplatio is always a matter of our receptivity to God's grace. Our task is to remove as many obstacles to God's Spirit as we can: our inner resistance, our fear of intimacy, our awareness of time, our desire to control the process, and our self-concern. We must remain lovingly attentive to God and experience the desire for interior silence. As we feel God drawing us into deeper awareness of his divine presence, we gradually abandon our intellectual activity and let ourselves be wooed into his embrace. The experience resembles that of lovers holding each other in wordless silence or of a sleeping child resting in the arms of its mother.

Though we might think that the movement of contemplatio is passive and uneventful, God's grace is truly at work in these moments, and the Holy Spirit is changing us from the inside without our awareness. In contemplatio our heart—the center of our being and the place where we are most truly ourselves—is humbly exposed to God. What happens within us during those moments is something beyond our control. Contemplatio slowly works at transforming our hearts, offering us a taste of the divine life that we are destined to share completely. Though there is often no sign of God at work in the silence, his invisible and unknowable presence is working to transform us at the deepest level.

Operatio: Faithful Witness in Daily Life

Through lectio divina, God's word shapes us and impacts our lives. After reading, reflecting, and praying over the word, we should be changed in some specific and concrete way. The changes we experience can be as simple as an adjusted attitude toward our work or a kindness to someone in need, or they can be as demanding as an urgency to change our career or reconcile with someone with whom we've been estranged. Operatio is this lived response to the inspired word.

Through lectio divina we evangelize ourselves, building bridges between the text and daily life. Every biblical text has a call or challenge to those who listen and respond to its sacred words. Operatio is the fruit that we bear from nurturing the word of God through our listening, reflecting, and praying. We gradually realize that the fruit of lectio divina is the fruit of the Spirit: "love, joy, peace, patience, kindness, generosity, faithfulness, gentleness, self-control" (Galatians 5:22-23). When we begin to notice this fruit in the way we live each day, we will know that the word of God is having its effect within us. In operatio, we become witnesses to God's kingdom and living members of Christ's body in the world.

Contemplatio and operatio grow together in the heart of one who prayerfully reads Scripture. The word of God draws us inward to that deep place inside ourselves where we find God; it also impels us outward to those places in need of the light of the divine word. Apart from operatio, contemplatio becomes passive introspection. Apart from contemplatio, operatio becomes superficial pragmatism.

Patience

Contemplatio cultivates compassion within us. It enables us to see the deepest meaning and significance of issues, problems, and events. Only when we have attained the understanding and compassion that contemplatio nurtures can our action in the world be a genuine work of God's Spirit. Throughout history many of

31

Christianity's most ardent activists have also been the most fervent contemplatives. Lectio divina helps us to be contemplative activists and active contemplatives.

Lectio divina is not so much a matter of interpreting a written text as it is of seeking Christ and learning to be his disciple. He is the living Word to whom all the other words of Scripture bear witness. Through listening to, reflecting on, and praying the Scripture, our hearts and minds are formed in the way of Christ. As we deepen our relationship with him and develop a personal bond with Christ, our actions become an imitation of Christ and vehicles of his presence to others.

As our discipleship deepens through lectio divina, we seek to be totally identified with Christ. We desire to live "in Christ," and we experience Christ working within us, with our lives animated by his Spirit. Rather than wanting to imitate Christ, we begin to experience Christ working through us, and our actions become more his work than our own. In contemplation, Christ prays within us, and in operatio, Christ becomes the doer of our actions. In this mystical bond with Christ, we see the true depth of discipleship that lectio divina can create within us.

Chapter Three

Lectio Divina for Advent: Year A

First Sunday of Advent

LECTIO

Be still and leave the commotion of the day as you prepare for your experience of the inspired word. Light the first Advent candle as a reminder to "walk in the light of the Lord" (Isaiah 2:5).

Inhale and exhale slowly, becoming aware of your breathing as you recognize each breath as a gift from God. Breathe in, being filled with the presence of God's Spirit. Breathe out, letting go of all that could distract you from this sacred time. Begin reading when you feel ready to hear God's voice.

ISAIAH 2:1-5

This is what Isaiah, son of Amoz, saw concerning Judah and Jerusalem.

In days to come,
the mountain of the Lord's house
    shall be established as the highest mountain
    and raised above the hills.
All nations shall stream toward it;
    many peoples shall come and say:
"Come, let us climb the Lord's mountain,
    to the house of the God of Jacob,
that he may instruct us in his ways,
    and we may walk in his paths."

For from Zion shall go forth instruction,
  and the word of the LORD from Jerusalem.
He shall judge between the nations,
  and impose terms on many peoples.
They shall beat their swords into plowshares
  and their spears into pruning hooks;
one nation shall not raise the sword against another,
  nor shall they train for war again.
O house of Jacob, come,
  let us walk in the light of the LORD!

Despite the looming threats to Jerusalem by her enemies, the proclamation of Isaiah turns to a vision of hope and peace. This ancient prophet expresses the hope that in the "days to come" (Isaiah 2:2), the height on which Jerusalem and its Temple stand will be the place to which all peoples will look up. All the nations will come to know the God of Israel, and the word of God will go forth from Jerusalem.

Isaiah visualizes how the people of all nations will stream toward the city of peace, where all will dwell in unity. Jerusalem will draw all the nations because of its fidelity to God and justice toward others. The swords and spears of warfare will be converted into plowshares and pruning hooks to provide grain and fruit. Nations will not go to battle or train for war again. Instruction in God's ways and walking in his path with the light of the Lord will bring the lasting peace for which all people dream.

The prophet's hope is based not in human persuasion or worldly power but in God's fidelity to his people and his dominion over the whole world. Through the coming of Jesus, the gospel of peace has been proclaimed to all the nations, yet we still await the fullness of God's kingdom. Isaiah's hope for mutual understanding of God's ways and lasting peace remains elusive. While this kind of hope involves total reliance on God, it also challenges us to expend serious effort in the present time working for peace on the personal, local, and international levels.

In Advent we break our normal routine and move into heightened alert to perceive more intensely the ways in which God is moving us toward that vision of peace that Isaiah so eloquently describes. But it takes more than just wishing and longing to make it a reality. The prophet pushes us beyond narrow self-interests and challenges us to work for peace while we look forward to the full coming of God's kingdom.

Let the words and images of the prophet sink in, and then when you are ready, begin reading the Gospel passage. Listen as the Gospel of Matthew impresses upon us the urgency of engaging in the struggle for peace and preparing our hearts for God's kingdom.

MATTHEW 24:37-44

Jesus said to his disciples: "As it was in the days of Noah, so it will be at the coming of the Son of Man. In those days before the flood, they were eating and drinking, marrying and giving in marriage, up to the day that Noah entered the ark. They did not know until the flood came and carried them all away. So will it be also at the coming of the Son of Man. Two men will be out in the field; one will be taken, and one will be left. Two women will be grinding at the mill; one will be taken, and one will be left. Therefore, stay awake! For you do not know on which day your Lord will come. Be sure of this: if the master of the house had known the hour of night when the thief was coming, he would have stayed awake and not let his house be broken into. So too, you also must be prepared, for at an hour you do not expect, the Son of Man will come."

⋏

The Scriptures for this First Sunday of Advent share the word "come" as their key theme. While we believe that God will come to us, the reading from Isaiah convinces us that we must also come to God. "Come, let us climb to the LORD's mountain / . . . Come, let us walk in the light of the LORD," the prophet exhorts (Isaiah 2:3, 5). In Advent we come to listen to his word of hope in the Scriptures. We come to worship him in the Eucharist. When we come to him, God can heal us, forgive us, console us, and renew us.

The Gospel tells us that God comes to meet us in Jesus Christ. He came among us at the time of his birth in Bethlehem long ago, but we await his glorious coming whenever and however that may be. Jesus tells his disciples, "At an hour you do not expect, the Son of Man will come" (Matthew 24:44). Christ will come in glory to fulfill all of God's promises and bring the fullness of God's kingdom. Therefore, as Advent reminds us, we must stay awake and be ready.

Advent is our yearly wake-up call, reminding us that we are not merely marking time with our lives, that our lives have an ultimate purpose and goal. The Scriptures and images of this season shake us out of our routine and weariness and invite us to consider anew the great hope that our faith offers us. Advent tells us that salvation is near, that God's kingdom is at hand, that even now we participate in the life to come.

Jesus presents a series of short parables, urging his disciples to be vigilant. He first compares his glorious coming in the final days with the days of Noah. In the days before the flood, people were going about the daily activities of life—eating and drinking, marrying and giving their children in marriage. These are the good but all-consuming realities of ordinary existence. They were unprepared for the flood, which carried them away. A second comparison depicts people out in the field and grinding grain, contributing to the normal work of life. The men working the crops and the women at the mill are outwardly no different, but one is ready for the kingdom and the other is not. The final parable urges disciples to live like the master of the house who stays vigilant and prepares for the thief in the night.

Jesus clearly does not urge us to quit the tasks of ordinary life. Rather, he urges us to have an interior awareness of his continual coming. He wants us to live as if he is coming in glory today. Constant readiness means being attentive to the many ways that he is present to us. If we are not attentive to Christ when we are eating and drinking, loving our spouse and raising our children, plowing the field and grinding grain, then we will be caught unprepared for the coming of the Son of Man in glory. We cannot prepare for salvation at the last minute because we do not know when the last minute will be. Constant vigilance at every moment is the stance of the Christian life and the perennial reminder of the Advent season.

MEDITATIO

ᴧ

The challenge of meditatio is to continue reflecting on the scriptural narratives until they become a mirror in which we see our own reflection. Recognize within the text your own temptations, sins, challenges, and failures.

- Isaiah urges us to come to God—to climb the Lord's mountain and to walk in his light (2:3, 5). How do you come to God? Do you come totally and entirely, ready to experience his presence and receive his renewing grace?

- Isaiah says that the nations "shall beat their swords into plowshares and their spears into pruning hooks" (2:4). What spiritual practices prepare you for the struggle to wage peace? How can you promote peace among people this season?

- People without hope are locked into their own world and are unable to imagine one that is different. What signs of hope do you see around you that help you realize that the world can be different?

- The three brief parables of Matthew's Gospel focus on the forgetfulness that can occur amid the many ordinary activities of life. We always have too much to do and not enough time to do it. How can you become more spiritually aware this season in order to rediscover life's purpose and passion?

- When Jesus said, "At an hour you do not expect, the Son of Man will come" (Matthew 24:44), he was teaching his disciples to live in light of the future. Why is it foolish and dangerous to speculate about the time of the future coming of Christ?

ORATIO

After listening and reflecting on the word of God, respond to that word with heartfelt and embodied prayer. Ask God to make you ready for the coming of Christ. Begin with this prayer and continue to pray as your heart directs you:

Saving Lord, I wait in joyful hope for your coming in glory. You teach me to always be ready though I cannot know the day of your coming. Keep me watchful and prepared so that I will be found serving the needs of your kingdom when you return in glory.

CONTEMPLATIO

Place yourself in God's presence, imagining Christ coming to meet you. Remain for a period of prolonged silence. If your mind drifts, repeat in quiet the ancient words "Come, Lord Jesus."

OPERATIO

Consider how God is transforming your heart through this experience of lectio divina. How are you more hopeful after having prayerfully reflected on these Scriptures of Advent? How will you use this Advent to prepare yourself for the coming of the Lord?

Second Sunday of Advent

LECTIO

Light the second Advent candle to help sanctify and purify the space that you have chosen to hear God's word. Call upon the same Holy Spirit who inspired the sacred writers to fill your heart and kindle in you the fire of divine love.

Read aloud, vocalizing the words of the text so that you not only read with your eyes but speak with your lips and hear with your ears. Listen deeply to God's word in your heart.

ISAIAH 11:1-10

On that day, a shoot shall sprout from the stump of Jesse,
    and from his roots a bud shall blossom.
The spirit of the LORD shall rest upon him:
    a spirit of wisdom and of understanding,
a spirit of counsel and of strength,
    a spirit of knowledge and of fear of the LORD,
    and his delight shall be the fear of the LORD.
Not by appearance shall he judge,
    nor by hearsay shall he decide,
but he shall judge the poor with justice,
    and decide aright for the land's afflicted.
He shall strike the ruthless with the rod of his mouth,
    and with the breath of his lips he shall slay the wicked.
Justice shall be the band around his waist,

and faithfulness a belt upon his hips.
Then the wolf shall be a guest of the lamb,
   and the leopard shall lie down with the kid;
the calf and the young lion shall browse together,
   with a little child to guide them.
The cow and the bear shall be neighbors,
   together their young shall rest;
   the lion shall eat hay like the ox.
The baby shall play by the cobra's den,
   and the child lay his hand on the adder's lair.
There shall be no harm or ruin on all my holy mountain;
   for the earth shall be filled with knowledge of the LORD,
   as water covers the sea.
On that day, the root of Jesse,
   set up as a signal for the nations,
the Gentiles shall seek out,
   for his dwelling shall be glorious.

人

Isaiah never fails to summon God's people to hope and expectation in the face of dismal circumstances. The long line of Israel's kings has been decimated like once majestic trees chopped down in a forest. But out of the hacked-off trunk and roots of Jesse, the father of King David, a new shoot will grow. This future ruler will exemplify all that is best in royal power, all that the kings of David's lineage failed to embody. This ideal king will be anointed not only with oil but with God's spirit—a spirit that will bestow on him the qualities necessary to render good judgments, speak the truth, and protect the rights of the poor. He will strike the ruthless and the wicked, those who exploit the weak and vulnerable, with his faithful word.

The ideal ruler will establish an idyllic kingdom. The images of wild and dangerous animals existing together without threat or violence express the peace of the messianic age. Destruction and war, which were such a part of Israel's life through the centuries, will end, and the whole earth will know God. The evil and degradation of sin will be reversed. The upside-down world will be turned right side up.

Isaiah voices hope for a new king, a new age, and a new kingdom. The stump of Jesse will initiate a reign that will prove attractive for all the nations of the world. The early Christians knew that these hopes had achieved at least partial fulfillment in the coming of Jesus. A descendant of King David, Jesus was led by the Holy Spirit and so was endowed with great wisdom. He acted with justice and taught others to do the same. He took the side of the vulnerable and oppressed. He was a man of peace and declared peacemakers to be especially blessed. His reign is attractive to Gentiles, and all the world's nations look to him.

After quietly considering the hopes offered by Isaiah, begin reading the Gospel passage. You will move down the ages to the proclamation of John the Baptist preparing the people of Israel for the advent of God's kingdom. Read the Gospel account with new eyes, listening to God's word and imagining this fascinating scene.

MATTHEW 3:1-12

John the Baptist appeared, preaching in the desert of Judea and saying, "Repent, for the kingdom of heaven is at hand!"

45

It was of him that the prophet Isaiah had spoken when he said:

> A voice of one crying out in the desert,
> Prepare the way of the Lord,
>   make straight his paths.

John wore clothing made of camel's hair and had a leather belt around his waist. His food was locusts and wild honey. At that time Jerusalem, all Judea, and the whole region around the Jordan were going out to him and were being baptized by him in the Jordan River as they acknowledged their sins.

When he saw many of the Pharisees and Sadducees coming to his baptism, he said to them, "You brood of vipers! Who warned you to flee from the coming wrath? Produce good fruit as evidence of your repentance. And do not presume to say to yourselves, 'We have Abraham as our father.' For I tell you, God can raise up children to Abraham from these stones. Even now the ax lies at the root of the trees. Therefore every tree that does not bear good fruit will be cut down and thrown into the fire. I am baptizing you with water, for repentance, but the one who is coming after me is mightier than I. I am not worthy to carry his sandals. He will baptize you with the Holy Spirit and fire. His winnowing fan is in his hand. He will clear his threshing floor and gather his wheat into his barn, but the chaff he will burn with unquenchable fire."

人

"Prepare the way of the Lord, / make straight his paths." These words of Isaiah (40:3) offered hope to the people of God in exile for their return to their land. The Gospel writer uses these prophetic words to describe the ministry of John the Baptist. He is the last of the great prophets to prepare the way for the coming of Israel's Messiah. He knows that the long exile of God's people will not be complete until the shoot "from the stump of Jesse" (Isaiah 11:1) offers God's salvation to the world.

John appears in the desert of Judea, along the banks of the Jordan River, to awaken Israel to what God is about to do. Purified by his own listening to God's word in the desert, John cuts through hypocrisy and sinfulness to make a straight path through the hearts of God's people. His message is "Repent, for the kingdom of heaven is at hand!" (Matthew 3:2). In the English translation, we miss the radical demands implied in this exhortation. Repentance is more than just being sorry about a particular action and resolving not to repeat it. The Hebrew word for "repent" implies turning around, changing the direction of one's life. The Greek word implies a radical change of mind and heart. Repentance involves a reordering of one's life, the profound transformation expressed by immersion in the waters of the Jordan.

Passing through the Jordan River was the last step for the Israelites in their transition from slavery in Egypt to new life in the Promised Land. For these followers of John, baptism in the Jordan represented a fresh beginning, a renewed acceptance of their commitment as the people of God. But John is adamant that this expression of repentance must not remain only in the realm of ritual and personal feeling. He insists, "Produce good fruit as evidence of your repentance" (Matthew 3:8). Repentance is a practical matter, made evident by the fruit of good deeds and a repentant lifestyle. Preparing the way for the Lord means laying the ax of conversion to the roots of any arrogant superiority or intolerance in our hearts. "The one who is coming" will separate the good grains of wheat from the chaff, baptizing "with the Holy Spirit and fire" (3:11).

John's fiery message is harsh as he speaks in shocking ways to startle his audience into action. Yet many found his message fascinating; people from the whole region went out to hear him and be baptized by him. This prophet of the desert clothed in camel's hair attracted people because he lived so authentically. He was confident of his purpose and his life had a clear mission. He was a compelling witness because he lived completely and totally what he proclaimed. People were drawn to him, not just in admiration, but to examine their own lives to see if such genuine sincerity and commitment to God's purposes could actually be lived.

MEDITATIO

Spend some time reflecting on the Scripture passages you have read, allowing them to interact with your own world of memories, questions, ideas, and concerns until you are aware of the personal messages the texts offer to you.

- Isaiah speaks about a world that has no hunger or harm, no need to devour, no yearning for brutal control, no desire to dominate. How does this vision of God's kingdom offer you hope for the future?

- Isaiah lists the gifts of the Spirit to be conferred on the Messiah. These gifts are bestowed on all Christians at baptism and confirmation. Which of the gifts of the Spirit can you claim today to do God's work?

- God's kingdom has already come in Jesus, yet his reign is not yet complete in the world, so we pray, "Thy kingdom come." In what ways does the coming of Jesus fulfill the prophecies of Isaiah about the coming king? Which parts of Isaiah's vision are yet to be completed?

- What is the essence of John the Baptist's call to "repent" (Matthew 3:2)? Why does he use the image of a fruitful tree to signify a repentant life?

- John had no patience for insincerity and hypocrisy. Why are people attracted to those who are genuinely authentic, whose purpose and mission in life are clear from what they say and do? What do you need to do to move in a direction of a more authentic life?

ORATIO

After listening and reflecting on the word of God, respond to that word with heartfelt and embodied prayer. Let this prayer be an incentive to continue with your own:

God of our ancestors, you prepared the world for the coming of your Son through the preaching of Isaiah and the call of John the Baptist to repentance. Help me turn away from sin and turn my heart to you so that I may bear fruit worthy of your kingdom.

Continue to pray in whatever words your heart directs.

CONTEMPLATIO

Imaginatively place yourself in the silence of the desert with John the Baptist. There is a mysterious beauty to the desert that can calm our inner noise and invite us into the stark presence of the Holy One. Spend some moments there, letting God gradually work deep within your heart so that you can orient your life totally to him.

OPERATIO

The experience of lectio divina always has some transforming effect on our lives. In the end, repentance is a practical matter—producing the good fruit that God wants. What practical result is God asking of you as evidence of your repentance?

Third Sunday of Advent

LECTIO

The joyful expectation of Advent is particularly emphasized by the Scripture readings of this Sunday. Light the rose-colored candle of the Advent wreath as you separate this time and space from the rest of your day so that you may be ready to truly hear the words of these inspired texts.

Highlight, underline, circle, and mark up the text as a way to focus on your reading. This will help you to pay attention in a new way as you read.

ISAIAH 35:1-6A, 10

The desert and the parched land will exult;
 the steppe will rejoice and bloom.
They will bloom with abundant flowers,
 and rejoice with joyful song.
The glory of Lebanon will be given to them,
 the splendor of Carmel and Sharon;
they will see the glory of the LORD,
 the splendor of our God.
Strengthen the hands that are feeble,
 make firm the knees that are weak,
say to those whose hearts are frightened:
 Be strong, fear not!
Here is your God,

 he comes with vindication;
with divine recompense
 he comes to save you.
Then will the eyes of the blind be opened,
 the ears of the deaf be cleared;
then will the lame leap like a stag,
 then the tongue of the mute will sing.

Those whom the LORD has ransomed will return
 and enter Zion singing,
 crowned with everlasting joy;
they will meet with joy and gladness,
 sorrow and mourning will flee.

∧

Isaiah uses his poetic vision and literary skills to anticipate a coming time when all creation will be healed and restored to well-being. He begins by evoking the sterility of nature with a triad: desert, parched land, and steppe. This austere landscape expresses the desolation of God's people. Yet the prophet proclaims that this arid land will exult, rejoice with song, and bloom with flowers. The triad of barrenness is overshadowed by a triad of fertility: Lebanon, Carmel, and Sharon. These are the lands with the richest soil, expressing the full generative nature of creation. God's rehabilitation of the land will be such that the crops will grow and the ground will bring forth vegetation, so much so that the land itself will break out in singing, rejoicing in God's glorious splendor.

 The prophet continues his vision of restoration by evoking a triad of disabled humans: hands that are feeble, knees that are weak, and hearts that are frightened. These disabled ones are unable to live according to their potential until God intervenes. Then strength will replace feebleness, hope will replace despair, and confidence will replace fear. The people know that their God is coming and will save them. He will water the land, right the wrong, heal the sick, and restore life to its potential. As the result of God's saving vindication, the blind will see, the deaf will hear, the lame will leap, and the mute will sing.

The vision that Isaiah offers God's people is dominated by great joy. God has ransomed his people, and they are returning to a fully restored Zion. First, he says, the land will rejoice, then the disabled will rejoice at their restoration to wholeness, and finally, those ransomed from captivity will rejoice. The place of God's dwelling will be fully restored and God's people will enter singing for joy.

Although Isaiah's poetic vision is a promise of God's ultimate purpose for creation and humanity, we can see it breaking into the world whenever God replaces fear with confidence, desolation with rejoicing, and despair with hope. When you have allowed the joyful hope of the prophet's words to penetrate your heart, prepare to listen carefully to the words of Matthew's Gospel.

MATTHEW 11:2-11

When John the Baptist heard in prison of the works of the Christ, he sent his disciples to Jesus with this question, "Are you the one who is to come, or should we look for another?" Jesus said to them in reply, "Go and tell John what you hear and see: the blind regain their sight, the lame walk, lepers are cleansed, the deaf hear, the dead are raised, and the poor have the good news proclaimed to them. And blessed is the one who takes no offense at me."

As they were going off, Jesus began to speak to the crowds about John, "What did you go out to the desert to see? A reed swayed by the wind? Then what did you go out to see? Someone dressed in fine clothing? Those who wear fine clothing are in royal palaces. Then why did you go out? To see a prophet? Yes, I tell you, and more than a prophet. This is the one about whom it is written:

> Behold, I am sending my messenger ahead of you;
> he will prepare your way before you.

Amen, I say to you, among those born of women there has been none greater than John the Baptist; yet the least in the kingdom of heaven is greater than he."

⅄

The Gospel passage reintroduces John the Baptist, who sends his disciples to Jesus with the same question that we must ask: Is Jesus "the one who is to come" or not? (Matthew 11:3). Jesus' reply back to John urges us to learn to see and recognize the same signs of his messianic coming.

In this scene John is in prison as a result of his mission of calling Israel to repentance. Perhaps he has become less confident that Jesus is the Messiah due to his own imprisonment, the increasing opposition to Jesus, the delay of God's judgment upon sin, and the oppressive religious and political leaders. The response of Jesus tells John's disciples to report what they "hear," Jesus' teachings and proclamation of the kingdom, and what they "see," the wondrous deeds of Jesus (Matthew 11:4). The implication is that each person must come to his or her own conclusion about whether Jesus is the one for whom they are waiting.

The list of messianic signs indicates that Jesus is fulfilling the prophecies of Isaiah and confirms that he is "the one who is to come." He is bringing wholeness to people: sight, mobility, cleanliness, hearing, life, and dignity are given to people who did not have them. By proclaiming the kingdom both in word and deed, Jesus is connecting people to God. Those who are attentive to these messianic signs will be "blessed" (Matthew 11:6) and realize the presence of salvation made known in Jesus the Messiah.

Jesus asks the crowd three times why they went out into the desert, the place of listening for God's word. What did they go to see? What drove them? Looking into our hearts to see what drives us, what we really want, is not an easy task. God's people were not looking for an unstable reed or a finely dressed ruler. They were looking for a real prophet, one who speaks the word of God, confronts the abuses of those who live in palaces, condemns sin and injustice, and points to wholeness and redemption. What they desired and what they found was John the Baptist as the path to Jesus, the one who would restore what was lost and connect people to God and his salvation.

MEDITATIO

The two Advent prophets, Isaiah and John the Baptist, speak the word of God and point to the coming of Christ. Let their words deepen your joyful anticipation as you reflect and meditate on these verses of Scripture.

- On this Gaudete (Rejoice) Sunday, expressed by the rose candle, what in these Scriptures makes you want to rejoice?

- Isaiah invites us to be filled with joy and gladness and to express it in singing and rejoicing, even when all seems desolate. The very expectation that the parched wasteland will yield fragrant blooms begins to bring it into being. The exiles were to enter into the ruined city singing for joy before seeing concrete signs of restoration. In what ways does Isaiah's exhortation express the meaning of genuine hope for you?

- Isaiah proclaims, "Here is your God, / he comes with vindication; / with divine recompense / he comes to save you" (35:4). In Isaiah's context, salvation is the deliverance of God's people from captivity, opposition, and conflict. It is both material and spiritual. It brings about perfect peace and a renewed relationship with God and other persons. In what ways does the salvation offered by Jesus both include and surpass the salvation of which Isaiah speaks?

- The examples of people who suffer forms of physical impairment in Isaiah's message and in Matthew's Gospel represent the entire human race, for we are all in some way impaired, and each of us longs for restoration. What healing and wholeness do you desire?

- Even though Jesus called John the Baptist the greatest of the prophets, he also said, "The least in the kingdom of heaven is greater than he" (Matthew 11:11). Those on whom salvation has dawned, who have seen and heard Jesus the Messiah, exceed John in what they have received and in what they are called to give. In what ways has this privilege been given to you?

ORATIO

人

The prophets want you to see the signs of God's saving presence around you. Ask God for a deep trust and confident expectation of his coming salvation. Let these words be your prayer starter:

Jesus, I believe that you are the one to come and that there is no need to wait for another. Through your words and deeds, I have come to know that you are the Messiah who has come to save the world. Help me with my struggles with doubt, and let me place my trust in you.

Continue to pray whatever words well up from the depths of your heart.

CONTEMPLATIO

人

Remain in restful quiet, experiencing the joyful anticipation evoked by these Scriptures. Open yourself to receive whatever spiritual gifts God desires to give you during these moments as you place your trust in the coming of Christ.

OPERATIO

Consider the transforming effects of your lectio divina as you journey through Advent and the ways that God is changing your heart. In what way this week can you express the joyful spirit signified by the rose-colored candle?

Fourth Sunday of Advent

LECTIO

⅄

Light the fourth candle of the Advent wreath or sit in the presence of the Christmas crèche with Joseph and Mary to help you focus on God's living word. Call upon the Holy Spirit to enlighten your eyes and your heart as you read the sacred texts.

Begin reading these familiar texts as if for the first time, trying to let go of your own presumptions so that you can listen to God speaking to you anew.

ISAIAH 7:10-14

The LORD spoke to Ahaz, saying: Ask for a sign from the LORD, your God; let it be deep as the netherworld, or high as the sky! But Ahaz answered, "I will not ask! I will not tempt the LORD!" Then Isaiah said: Listen, O house of David! Is it not enough for you to weary people, must you also weary my God? Therefore the Lord himself will give you this sign: the virgin shall conceive, and bear a son, and shall name him Emmanuel.

⅄

Isaiah has been trying to persuade King Ahaz not to ally God's people with corrupt and ruthless powers but to trust in the covenant and follow the way of the Lord. To back up his exhortation, Isaiah invites Ahaz to ask for a sign from God. But the king refuses to ask for a sign, not because he already trusts in God, but because a sign revealing the will of God would require him to change. The stance of Ahaz may be the place where we find ourselves this Advent. We refuse to look at the signs God offers us, declining the offer to see indications of God's will because of the change in our lives that such signs might require.

But despite the king's refusal, God provided the sign of Emmanuel through his prophet Isaiah. The prophecy spoke of the approaching birth of a new king, one who would assure the continuance of David's dynasty after a period of devastation. His birth and reign would bring restoration to the land and would be a signal that God was truly with his people. This prophecy of the reign of David's descendant over God's restored people did not find satisfactory fulfillment in the generations immediately following King Ahaz. Rather, the high ideals of these Emmanuel prophecies (Isaiah 7, 9, 11) became a messianic hope for a future age.

The mother of the future king is called "a young woman" in the Hebrew text, a maiden of marriageable age, but the Greek text of the Old Testament, the version more familiar to the early Christians, calls the woman "the virgin." In the Hebrew Scriptures, Israel and Jerusalem are often referred to as a young woman, and sometimes specifically as a virgin (Isaiah 37:22; Jeremiah 31:4). The later Jewish period saw in Isaiah's words a messianic prophecy and proposed that virgin Israel would give birth to the Messiah.

The title "Emmanuel" means "God-with-us." God's promise, "I will be with you," was made throughout Israel's history to patriarchs, kings, and prophets. In the birth of the Messiah, God's promise became effective and is forever being confirmed and fulfilled through the eternal reign of Christ.

The use of this text by Matthew in his Gospel expresses the Christian faith in the royal identity of Jesus and his birth from the Virgin Mary. Mary represents virgin Israel, implying that God's people cannot bring forth the Messiah from their own human history but only through the direct intervention of God. When you are ready, read the account of the coming of Christ from the Gospel according to Matthew.

MATTHEW 1:18-24

This is how the birth of Jesus Christ came about. When his mother Mary was betrothed to Joseph, but before they lived together, she was found with child through the Holy Spirit. Joseph her husband, since he was a righteous man, yet unwilling to expose her to shame, decided to divorce her quietly. Such was his intention when, behold, the angel of the Lord appeared to him in a dream and said, "Joseph, son of David, do not be afraid to take Mary your wife into your home. For it is through the Holy Spirit that this child has been conceived in her. She will bear a son and you are to name him Jesus, because he will save his people from their sins." All this took place to fulfill what the Lord had said through the prophet:

Behold, the virgin shall conceive and bear a son,
and they shall name him Emmanuel,

which means "God is with us." When Joseph awoke, he did as the angel of the Lord had commanded him and took his wife into his home.

人

This narrative at the beginning of Matthew's Gospel explains how the coming Messiah will be both Son of David and Son of God. Through the lineage of Joseph and his legal paternity, Jesus is Son of David; through the Holy Spirit and the virginal maternity of Mary, Jesus is Son of God. The obedient responses of both Joseph and Mary to the divine will were necessary for Christ's coming into the world. Through Joseph, Jesus' birth is placed in continuity with God's work through the ages, thus expressing God's consistent faithfulness; through Mary, his birth is shown to be a marvelously new divine action, thus expressing God's astonishing creativity.

In addressing Joseph as "son of David" (Matthew 1:20), the angel evoked the messianic prophecies of the future king from David's lineage. By bringing Mary into his home in marriage, assuming public responsibility for their child, and giving a name to the child, Joseph became the legal and adoptive father of Jesus. Because his father was of the line of David, Jesus legitimately became a descendant of David's royal lineage. Through Joseph, Jesus was able to be proclaimed as the Son of David, the Messiah of Israel.

Joseph's choices were agonizing. Mary and Joseph were "betrothed," a legally binding relationship for a year or more before the couple were to share the same home. The evidence spoke for itself. Joseph could only assume that Mary had relations with another man. Yet Joseph, out of love for Mary, chose to quietly divorce her without public accusation, trial, punishment, and shame. But the revelation in his dream cut short one painful choice and presented him with another: the choice to cooperate with the inconceivable grace of God. Joseph's life and his future were now out of his hands. Because Joseph followed God's will as revealed to him, his life entered the cosmic drama wherein heaven and earth met in the child of Mary's womb.

The text of Isaiah's Emmanuel prophecy proclaims and fortifies the belief of the Christian community in the messianic identity of Jesus and his wondrous conception through the Virgin Mary. The translation "God is with us" underlines the connection between the Old Testament and the New, the continuity between God's working through the ancient biblical tradition of Israel and God's new work in the coming of the Messiah. The fulfillment of this ancient passage in the coming of Jesus does not remove its significance in the tradition of Israel or imply the end of Israel's covenant with God. On the contrary, it demonstrates the oneness of God's saving plan for all people and his commitment to be with us always.

MEDITATIO

Let these Scriptures touch your heart by reflecting on them in light of your own experiences of trust and hope.

- Isaiah asked King Ahaz, "Is it not enough for you to weary people, must you also weary my God?" (Isaiah 7:13). In what ways do you feel weary during these last days of Advent? How can you transform your weariness into wonder?

- Like Ahaz, we are not interested in asking for a sign because we have our own alliances with power, wealth, and influence as provision for our security. In what ways do you refuse to look at the signs God offers you because of the change that such signs might require? What are some of the signs God wants to give to you?

- What did Emmanuel, "God is with us," mean for Isaiah in the eighth century before Christ? What did it mean for Matthew in his birth narrative? What does it mean today as you seek to follow Christ?

- In what ways do the prophecy of Isaiah and the narrative of Joseph and Mary show the continuity between the Old and New Testaments? How does the Gospel passage indicate an astounding newness?

- Although Luke's Gospel emphasizes the role of Mary in the coming of Jesus, Matthew's Gospel spotlights the response of Joseph to God's saving action in the world. What do you admire most about Joseph? What do his willing responses teach you about Advent trust?

ORATIO

It is God's grace at work within us that gives us a desire to pray. Respond to the word of God that you have heard by lifting up your voice to God and expressing the contents of your heart:

Jesus, Emmanuel, you come into our world as a manifestation of "God-with-us." Help me to believe that God is with me in the best and the worst of times. Renew my hope in your promises and give me trust, like Joseph, to live with confidence.

Continue your prayer by giving thanks for the ways in which you experience "God-with-us"

CONTEMPLATIO

When the words of prayer are no longer necessary or helpful, move into a wordless silence in the divine presence. Open your heart to God and repeat the words "Come, Emmanuel." Trust that God is working deep within you.

OPERATIO

God can manifest his presence to us in many ways if we are able to perceive the divine manifestations. The sign that God gave to Ahaz through his prophet Isaiah and the dreams God gave to Joseph are all manifestations of God's will and guiding presence. How can you be more aware of God's signs? Spend this week trying to perceive the signs of God's will in your own life.

Chapter Four

Lectio Divina for Advent: Year B

First Sunday of Advent

LECTIO

Light the first Advent candle as you quiet your inner spirit and free yourself from the distractions of the day. Kiss the text of Scripture as a sign of your reverence for the sacred page and your desire to receive its transforming message.

As you read, feel free to highlight, underline, circle, or mark up the text and commentary as a tool for interacting with the readings. You will find that these marks help you be attentive to details and remember the words during your encounter with God's word.

ISAIAH 63:16B-17, 19B; 64:2-7

You, LORD, are our father,
  our redeemer you are named forever.
Why do you let us wander, O LORD, from your ways,
  and harden our hearts so that we fear you not?
Return for the sake of your servants,
  the tribes of your heritage.
Oh, that you would rend the heavens and come down,
  with the mountains quaking before you,
while you wrought awesome deeds we could not hope for,
  such as they had not heard of from of old.
No ear has ever heard, no eye ever seen, any God but you
  doing such deeds for those who wait for him.
Would that you might meet us doing right,

that we were mindful of you in our ways!
Behold, you are angry, and we are sinful;
    all of us have become like unclean people,
    all our good deeds are like polluted rags;
we have all withered like leaves,
    and our guilt carries us away like the wind.
There is none who calls upon your name,
    who rouses himself to cling to you;
for you have hidden your face from us
    and have delivered us up to our guilt.
Yet, O LORD, you are our father;
    we are the clay and you the potter:
    we are all the work of your hands.

The essence of spirituality is waking up to the presence of God in our lives. God is always coming toward us; we must turn around and be aware of his coming. Isaiah expresses the lament of the people of Israel as they return to Jerusalem and view their destroyed Temple and city. God is "our father, our redeemer" (Isaiah 63:16), yet he has allowed his people to wander from his ways and to harden their hearts. As children are inclined to fault the parents when things go wrong, Israel blames God for their turning away. It was God's parental neglect, they claim, that made them stray and that hardened their hearts so that they didn't respect him. Yet despite their outrageous and shocking claims, they will wake up, acknowledge their infidelity, turn toward God, and trustingly say to him, "No ear has ever heard, no eye ever seen, any God but you / doing such deeds for those who wait for him" (64:3).

The returning exiles cry out above the internal noise of their own preoccupations and worries, "Oh, that you would rend the heavens and come down!" (Isaiah 63:19). All the questions and doubts, the pains and tensions that are expressed by God's people are lifted up in their passionate plea. Audacious in their hope, they plead for God to transform their present anguish and despair into the birth pangs of something entirely new. They implore God to work "deeds we could not hope for, / such as they had not heard of from of old" (64:2-3).

But God's people realize that they cannot recognize God's coming to them until they repent. They recognize that they are polluted like dirty laundry and blown away like withered leaves. They finally throw themselves upon God's mercy and confess their sins, clearing the way of any prideful thoughts that they can save themselves: "Yet, O LORD, you are our father; / we are the clay and you the potter: / we are all the work of your hands" (Isaiah 64:7).

God is the one who has formed them and who continually molds them. They are as helpless before him as the clay. This humble repentance opens their lives to the reentry of God's healing grace and divine forgiveness.

Through the coming of Jesus Christ, God does indeed "rend the heavens" and come down. The Lord came first to his people through the virgin womb of Mary, and he will come again when human history has run its course. When you are ready to listen, begin reading the Gospel of Mark as he urges us to take up the Advent stance of vigilant expectation.

MARK 13:33-37

Jesus said to his disciples: "Be watchful! Be alert! You do not know when the time will come. It is like a man traveling abroad. He leaves home and places his servants in charge, each with his own work, and orders the gatekeeper to be on the watch. Watch, therefore; you do not know when the lord of the house is coming, whether in the evening, or at midnight, or at cockcrow, or in the morning. May he not come suddenly and find you sleeping. What I say to you, I say to all: 'Watch!'"

In this final discourse, Jesus exhorts his disciples, "Be watchful! Be alert!" (Mark 13:33). Since it is impossible to know when the day of the Lord's coming might be, the call to all followers of Jesus, in the first century or the twenty-first century, is to live with an attitude of vigilance, alertness, and watchfulness so as not to be caught unprepared. We should live as if Christ might return at any moment and ask us to account for what we have done with our lives. But the discourse is not only a warning but also a joyous anticipation of the coming of the Lord, the blessed hope for which the whole Church longs and prays.

How does Jesus urge the disciples to live with this kind of expectant hope? He offers the parable of the home owner who puts his servants and gatekeepers in charge of his house. We are the servants and gatekeepers of the Lord's house before he returns. Notice that the servants continue to work as they anticipate the master's return and that the gatekeeper continues to keep watch. One takes a contemplative stance; the other, an active stance. Working while watching, watching while working—this must be the posture of every disciple. As followers of Jesus, we are active contemplatives and contemplative activists. Advent calls us to quiet ourselves with prayer and to engage ourselves in the work of God's kingdom.

MEDITATIO

Allow the book of your life and the book of Scripture to "dialogue" so that you come to understand the significance of these readings for you as you enter Advent.

- For some, this Advent is a season of joyful expectation; for others, it is a season of mournful memories of loved ones; for still others, it is a time of dreaded anxiety over the coming holidays. Identify your moods and emotions this season. What might be your unique challenge during this season?

- During Advent we remember the past with gratitude and look forward to the future with hope. Both our remembrance and our anticipation are centered on the coming of Christ. How does gratitude for Christ's first coming and confidence in his coming in glory affect the way you live in the present?

- Consider Isaiah's image of God as a potter. In what ways have you experienced yourself as clay in the hands of the divine potter. What does God want to reshape in your life this Advent?

- How can you be both a servant at work in the Lord's house and a gatekeeper keeping watch for his coming? What does it mean to you to integrate the contemplative and the active dimensions of life?

- Advent reminds us to live fully in the present while being aware that we stand on the edge of the future. How might your life be different if you truly lived with watchfulness, expectancy, and vigilance?

ORATIO

Pray to God in response to what you have discovered within yourself from your listening and reflection. You may begin with these words:

Lord of glory, may I keep my heart ready to meet you. Since I may come face-to-face with you any day, either through my own death or through your glorious return, keep me watchful, awake, and ready.

Continue to interact with God as one who knows you intimately, cares about you deeply, and accepts you unconditionally.

CONTEMPLATIO

⋏

Be present before God with expectation at this threshold of Advent. Let God work within you, molding you like clay in the hands of the divine potter. Open your heart to God's grace.

OPERATIO

⋏

Make an Advent commitment to God to listen and watch more closely for the movements of God in your life. How does your practice of lectio divina help you to live this way?

Second Sunday of Advent

LECTIO

Prepare your space for encountering God's word by lighting the second candle of the Advent wreath or by placing another symbol of Advent in front of you. Call upon the same Holy Spirit who inspired the sacred writers to fill your heart and kindle in you the fire of divine love.

Begin reading when you feel ready to hear God's voice. Read these familiar passages as if for the first time. Try not to bring your own presumptions to the text but listen to God speaking to you anew.

ISAIAH 40:1-5, 9-11

Comfort, give comfort to my people,
 says your God.
Speak tenderly to Jerusalem, and proclaim to her
  that her service is at an end,
  her guilt is expiated;
indeed, she has received from the hand of the LORD
  double for all her sins.

  A voice cries out:
In the desert prepare the way of the LORD!
  Make straight in the wasteland a highway for our God!
Every valley shall be filled in,

every mountain and hill shall be made low;
the rugged land shall be made a plain,
the rough country, a broad valley.
Then the glory of the LORD shall be revealed,
and all people shall see it together;
for the mouth of the LORD has spoken.

Go up on to a high mountain,
Zion, herald of glad tidings;
cry out at the top of your voice,
Jerusalem, herald of good news!
Fear not to cry out
and say to the cities of Judah:
Here is your God!
Here comes with power
the Lord GOD,
who rules by his strong arm;
here is his reward with him,
his recompense before him.
Like a shepherd he feeds his flock;
in his arms he gathers the lambs,
carrying them in his bosom,
and leading the ewes with care.

⋏

During Advent we relive the experience of our biblical ancestors as they awaited the manifestation of God. Isaiah, our prophet of Advent, was the prophet of Israel's exile, offering words of great hope, comfort, and consolation. From the captivity of God's people in Babylon, God announces through his prophet that he would bring them deliverance and forgiveness. God would bring them back to Jerusalem and offer them again an unmistakable experience of divine presence.

To a people mourning for their homeland, God commands, "Comfort, give comfort to my people" (Isaiah 40:1). God is removing the obstacles that have cut Israel off from God: "Proclaim to her / that her service is at an end, / her guilt is expiated" (40:2). Through repentance and divine forgiveness, God is releasing his people from their captives and restoring their blessings.

God's gracious reentry into the life of his outcast people is described as a grand procession through the desert. God exhorts, "In the desert prepare the way of the LORD!" (Isaiah 40:3). Just as God rescued the Israelites from Egypt in ancient days and brought them to their own land, so God will release his people from their bondage in Babylon and return them to Jerusalem. The ultimate purpose of the great turn of events is so that God's saving presence will be manifested to all people: "Then the glory of the LORD shall be revealed, / and all people shall see it together" (40:5).

The climactic announcement is reached as Jerusalem/Zion is called to proclaim God's imminent coming: "Here is your God!" (Isaiah 40:9). God's advent is elaborated with two contrasting images: God comes as the victorious warrior who rules with his strong arm and as the gentle shepherd who gathers the lambs in his arms. Both images of God were preserved and expanded in Israel's Scriptures.

Isaiah taught the Israelites that God was doing something new for them in every generation. The early Church looked to Isaiah's prophecy as the announcement of the Messiah's coming. After listening with the ear of your heart to Isaiah's proclamation of God's fidelity, you are ready to hear anew the prologue of Mark's Gospel. Trace the sign of the cross on your forehead, lips, and heart to prepare yourself to embrace God's word with your whole life.

MARK 1:1-8

The beginning of the gospel of Jesus Christ the Son of God. As it is written in Isaiah the prophet:

Behold, I am sending my messenger ahead of you;
he will prepare your way.
A voice of one crying out in the desert:
"Prepare the way of the Lord,
make straight his paths."

John the Baptist appeared in the desert proclaiming a baptism of repentance for the forgiveness of sins. People of the whole Judean countryside and all the inhabitants of Jerusalem were going out to him and were being baptized by him in the Jordan River as they acknowledged their sins. John was clothed in camel's hair, with a leather belt around his waist. He fed on locusts and wild honey. And this is what he proclaimed: "One mightier than I is coming after me. I am not worthy to stoop and loosen the thongs of his sandals. I have baptized you with water; he will baptize you with the Holy Spirit."

The beginning of the Gospel of Mark is abrupt, plunging us into the urgency of the time. There are no narratives of Jesus' conception and birth as in the Gospels of Matthew and Luke and no poetic prologue as in the Gospel of John. Mark's Gospel begins with quotations from the Old Testament, creating a mood of expectancy. Though attributed to Isaiah, the passage comes from several places in the Law and the prophets of Israel: from Exodus 23:20—"See, I am sending an angel before you"; from Malachi 3:1—"I am sending my messenger to prepare the way"; and from Isaiah 40:3—"A voice cries out: / In the desert prepare the way of the LORD!" These words from the ancient Scriptures indicate that the coming of Jesus Christ has been prepared by God through the history of ancient Israel and is now being fulfilled.

Mark's Gospel sets the stage for Jesus by first describing the adult ministry of John the Baptist, the messenger sent to prepare for Christ's coming. This rugged prophet is not an easy character to fit into a festive season. There are no Christmas carols about John the Baptist, and he's not the kind of guest we'd invite to a holiday party. His message of repentance is not the kind of thing quoted in greeting cards. But he is the Advent patron, the one who prepares the way and sets lives straight for the Savior's coming.

John the Baptist invites God's people into the quiet of the desert, challenging them to look carefully at their lives and repent of their sins. He asks them to prepare their hearts so that they will recognize the Messiah. John was evidently saying something that people needed to hear, for "the whole Judean countryside and all the inhabitants of Jerusalem were going out to him" (Mark 1:5).

John brings the people to the Jordan River, "proclaiming a baptism of repentance for the forgiveness of sins" (Mark 1:4). Isaiah's "way of the LORD" (40:3) runs through the desert and through the waters. This was the path of the Israelites on their way to the Promised Land; it was the way for God's exiled people as they returned to the land from Babylon; and so the same pathway makes God's people ready for the advent of Israel's Messiah. In these historical events of Israel, passage through the desert and through the Jordan River expressed repentance, forgiveness, and a renewed relationship with God. So too, as John prepares the way for Jesus, we see that the way to salvation runs through the desert and through the waters.

Like all the prophets of old, John speaks to us today. We need to hear John's sober call to a baptism of repentance in the barrenness of our own desert. We need to hear the message of forgiveness and to know that we can draw near to God. We can make our hearts ready for the coming of Christ by turning away from all that could separate us from him. The hour of God's grace is upon us. The moment of salvation is now.

MEDITATIO

The ministry of God's prophets is proclaimed in the Church's liturgy for our meditation and contemplation. Consider how Isaiah and John the Baptist prepare you for the coming of God's Messiah.

- Isaiah's opening cry, "Comfort, give comfort to my people. . . . / Speak tenderly to Jerusalem" (40:1, 2) made hope come alive again for God's people in exile. How do the prophet's words make you feel during this time of Advent?

- Isaiah's contrasting images of divine warrior and gentle shepherd both describe the coming of God to his people. Why was it important for Israel to preserve both images? Why are both of these images helpful for you in anxious times?

- One of the earliest designations of the Christian movement was "the Way" (Acts 9:2; 19:23). How does the beginning of Mark's Gospel indicate that the ministry of Jesus would be a new way? In what sense is your Christian life a path or a way?

- The way of salvation runs through the desert. Why is the desert an important context for Advent? In what sense can you go to the desert during these days?

- What is the meaning of repentance? Why is repentance the essential preparation for the coming of Jesus?

ORATIO

Use the words, images, and emotions from your lectio and meditatio as the foundation of your prayerful response to God. Come before God with repentance and with new hope. You may begin your prayer with these words:

God of our ancestors, you give me words of comfort and hope during this season. Prepare the way for the coming of your Son by moving me to repent so that you can offer me your gracious forgiveness. Help me to trust in your promises and believe in your salvation.

Continue voicing the prayer that issues from your heart as you ponder the call of God's prophets.

CONTEMPLATIO

The quiet harshness of the desert helps us realize that words fall into silence before the living God. As the words of your prayer become inadequate to express your heart, just remain in silence before the majesty of God who reveals himself in the sparse wilderness.

OPERATIO

John the Baptist calls God's people to a baptism of repentance in anticipation of the Messiah. Repentance is a radical change of mind and heart as well as a reordering of one's life. What is one way that I can express repentance this week so as to experience the fruit of God's forgiveness?

Third Sunday of Advent

LECTIO

Light the third candle (the rose candle) of the Advent wreath. Call upon the Holy Spirit to guide your listening to these sacred texts and to open your heart as you read.

Vocalize the words of the text so that you not only read them with your eyes but express them with your lips and hear them with your ears. Listen for the word of the Lord.

ISAIAH 61:1-2A, 10-11

The spirit of the Lord GOD is upon me,
    because the LORD has anointed me;
he has sent me to bring glad tidings to the poor,
    to heal the brokenhearted,
to proclaim liberty to the captives
    and release to the prisoners,
to announce a year of favor from the LORD
    and a day of vindication by our God.

I rejoice heartily in the LORD,
    in my God is the joy of my soul;
for he has clothed me with a robe of salvation
    and wrapped me in a mantle of justice,
like a bridegroom adorned with a diadem,
    like a bride bedecked with her jewels.

As the earth brings forth its plants,
and a garden makes its growth spring up,
so will the Lord GOD make justice and praise
spring up before all the nations.

The speaker in this prophetic text may be an individual person or
the community of God's people personified. In fact, in the Isaian tradition, this ambiguity is probably intentional; the speaker is set forth
as a model for both individuals and the community who respond
to the divine call to be agents of God's compassionate reign. Like
the Servant of earlier Isaian texts, the speaker is the ideal prophet,
the ideal Jerusalem, God's ideal people, and the Messiah.

Most important, the speaker is anointed and empowered by the
Spirit of God: "The spirit of the Lord GOD is upon me, / because
the LORD has anointed me" (Isaiah 61:1). Throughout the Old
Testament, weak and ordinary human beings, such as prophets,
judges, and kings, rise up to accomplish daunting tasks through the
empowerment of God's Spirit. As a representational figure of the
ideal individual and the community of God, the speaker is called
to accomplish God's divinely appointed work in the new situation
of God's people after the exile.

The prophetic text looks to the total salvation of God's people—bodily and spiritually, individually and socially. Isaiah has the
imagination and courage to speak not only about what is happen-
ing but about what should happen. Those anointed by God's Spirit
must be agents of God's merciful healing to those who are broken
and oppressed. They must announce with words and deeds that
the time has arrived for God to restore the conditions of justice

and peace that characterize the divine reign. That means good news for the poor, consolation for those who have given up hope, freedom to prisoners of every kind, and a time of God's favor for all who have waited.

Despite the work of God's anointed, this fullness of life of which the prophet speaks is not a human accomplishment. God is the one who causes his people to rejoice, covering them with garments of salvation and justice. The joy of God's people in Jerusalem will be like that of a newly married bride and groom in whose love is the promise of new life. What God has planted will flourish and blossom, brought forth from the earth by God's saving power. So there is every reason to rejoice in hope.

The calling to bear good news through the anointing of God's Spirit is the task of the true prophet. While the false prophets of Israel were unmasked by their commitment to self-gain, genuine prophets are validated by being free from preoccupation with self. In the New Testament, John the Baptist is called to this prophetic task, always pointing to Jesus and insisting that Jesus must increase while he decreases. And ultimately this text speaks of Jesus himself, the Messiah through whom God will make justice and praise spring up before all the nations of the world.

JOHN 1:6-8, 19-28

A man named John was sent from God. He came for testimony, to testify to the light, so that all might believe through him. He was not the light, but came to testify to the light.

And this is the testimony of John. When the Jews from Jerusalem sent priests and Levites to him to ask him, "Who are you?" he admitted and did not deny it, but admitted, "I am not the Christ." So they asked him, "What are you then? Are you Elijah?" And he said, "I am not." "Are you the Prophet?" He answered, "No." So they said to him, "Who are you, so we can give an answer to those who sent us? What do you have to say for yourself?" He said:

"I am *the voice of one crying out in the desert,
make straight the way of the Lord,*

as Isaiah the prophet said." Some Pharisees were also sent. They asked him, "Why then do you baptize if you are not the Christ or Elijah or the Prophet?" John answered them, "I baptize with water; but there is one among you whom you do not recognize, the one who is coming after me, whose sandal strap I am not worthy to untie." This happened in Bethany across the Jordan, where John was baptizing.

人

John the Baptist is a person of self-effacing honesty and humility who knows that his role in God's plan is a preparatory one. He is sent from God "to testify to the light, so that all might believe through him" (John 1:7). As the precursor of Jesus, John wants to make sure that his role is not mistaken for that of Jesus. He states emphatically to those who inquire of him, "I am not the Christ" (1:20). He replies with the words of Isaiah, saying that he is the one crying out in the desert, urging people to prepare for the Lord's coming. He is not even worthy to take on the role of a servant taking off the sandals of the master. Everything that John says about himself prepares for his testimony about Jesus.

All of us must answer the questions of the religious leaders from Jerusalem: "Who are you? What do you have to say for yourself?" We can answer those questions in many ways, citing our successes, relationships, occupation, degrees, and awards. But we ought to take a clue from the response of John who said, "I am not the Christ." John the Baptist knew that it was not about him or what he had done. Rather, it was—and is—about Jesus.

John's role in God's plan offers us the foundation of a healthy and honest spiritual life. We are not the Messiah. Our life task is to prepare always for the coming of Christ: when history has run its course, at the moment of our own death, in the Sacrament of the Eucharist, and in the manifold ways that he comes to us each day. We are not the light. Our role is to testify to the Light of the world. It's not that God expects us to dress in camel skins, eat locusts, and live in the desert. But by the words we speak and the way in which we live, we are called to point others to Christ.

MEDITATIO

Reflect on these texts so that they may become an instrument of hope and healing for you in the days of Advent. Consider how you can allow the printed text to become the living word of our saving God.

- Isaiah's text expresses the role of the ideal prophet and the ideal people of God. In what sense can this text be fulfilled completely and perfectly only in Jesus Christ?

- In the Sacraments of Baptism and Confirmation, all disciples are anointed by the Holy Spirit and sent to do the work of Christ in the world. How does Isaiah's text direct you in your desire to be a Spirit-led instrument of God's saving grace in the world?

- How does John the Baptist demonstrate a proper understanding of his own Spirit-endowed strengths as well as his limitations? What can you learn from John's self-understanding?

- The mission of John the Baptist is now in our hands. As prophets and evangelizers, we point the way to Christ. What are some ways in which people today can guide others to him?

- In the third week of Advent, Isaiah urges us to "rejoice heartily in the Lord" (61:10). What reasons do these Scriptures offer you to rejoice and be glad?

ORATIO

Using the words, images, and emotions from the texts that you have reflected on, offer your response to God's word. You may begin your prayer with these words:

Come, Holy Spirit, and empower me to be an instrument of liberation, healing, and justice in the places where I live and work. Keep me humble so that my words and deeds may always point to Christ. To him be the kingdom, the power, and the glory forever.

Continue your prayer with words that convey the sentiments of your heart. Try to express your prayer with a zeal worthy of the God who liberates you from the captivity of falsehood and despair.

CONTEMPLATIO

Go into the desert of your imagination and ask God to purify your desires. Pray for the grace of humility and ask God to form you into a transparent witness to Christ. Give God the control and let God's Spirit work within you in whatever way is needed.

OPERATIO

Go into the desert of your imagination and ask God to purify your desires. Pray for the grace of humility and ask God to form you into a transparent witness to Christ. Give God the control and let God's Spirit work within you in whatever way is needed.

As the forerunner of Christ, John the Baptist prepared the way of the Lord in order to show God's people how to get ready for Christ's coming. What is one way you could take on the role of John the Baptist this week, showing the way for others to prepare for the coming of Christ?

Fourth Sunday of Advent

LECTIO

Prepare your space for encountering God's living word in Scripture. Light the fourth candle of Advent or place some other visible symbol before you to help you focus on the texts. Call upon the Holy Spirit to enlighten your eyes and your mind as you read the Sacred Scriptures.

Begin reading when you are prepared to encounter God through the words of the sacra pagina.

2 SAMUEL 7:1-5, 8B-12, 14A, 16

When King David was settled in his palace, and the LORD had given him rest from his enemies on every side, he said to Nathan the prophet, "Here I am living in a house of cedar, while the ark of God dwells in a tent!" Nathan answered the king, "Go, do whatever you have in mind, for the LORD is with you." But that night the LORD spoke to Nathan and said: "Go, tell my servant David, 'Thus says the LORD: Should you build me a house to dwell in?

"'It was I who took you from the pasture and from the care of the flock to be commander of my people Israel. I have been with you wherever you went, and I have destroyed all your enemies before you. And I will make you famous like the great ones of the earth. I will fix a place for my people Israel; I will plant them so that they may dwell in their place without further disturbance. Neither shall the wicked continue to afflict them as they did of old, since the time I first appointed judges over my people Israel. I will give you rest from all your enemies. The LORD also reveals to you that he will establish a house for you. And when your time comes and you rest with your ancestors, I will raise up your heir after you, sprung from your loins, and I will make his kingdom firm. I will be a father to him, and he shall be a son to me. Your house and your kingdom shall endure forever before me; your throne shall stand firm forever.'"

The prophecy of Nathan to King David focuses our attention on how God wishes to dwell among his people. David had established his royal city in Jerusalem, defeated Israel's enemies, placed the ark of the covenant in a tent, united all the tribes under his rule, and built a palace for himself. He assumed that his next step would be to build a splendid temple for God.

Yet through his prophet, God asks, "Should you build me a house to dwell in?" (2 Samuel 7:5). Up until this time, God has been on the move with the Israelites, his presence expressed through a portable tabernacle that they carried with them wherever they sojourned. The one who identified himself as "I am who am" (Exodus 3:14), as being uncontainable, uncontrollable, and recognized by liberating actions, cannot permanently dwell in a house made with human hands.

Through Nathan's prophecy, David is surprised to discover that God's plans for him are far greater than his plans for God. God first reminds David that he has been with him along the way, taking him from the pasture with his sheep and making him the commander of Israel. He promises David a fixed place to live for his people and rest from his enemies, and finally, he promises to establish the kingdom of David forever. The oracle is built around a play on the word "house," which can mean either "temple" or "dynasty." David will not build God a house-temple; rather, God will build David a house-dynasty. God will give David an eternal lineage, and his reign will be established without end.

This divine covenant with David is the root of Israel's messianic hope. God's promise is unconditional: "Your house and your kingdom shall endure forever before me; your throne shall stand firm forever" (2 Samuel 7:16). The double assertion of the word "forever" shows that God's pledge is permanent and irrevocable. There is a future offspring of David who will bring God's justice and peace and whose reign will never end. This is the house that God desires. This is how God wishes to dwell among his people.

LUKE 1:26-38

The angel Gabriel was sent from God to a town of Galilee called Nazareth, to a virgin betrothed to a man named Joseph, of the house of David, and the virgin's name was Mary. And coming to her, he said, "Hail, full of grace! The Lord is with you." But she was greatly troubled at what was said and pondered what sort of greeting this might be. Then the angel said to her, "Do not be afraid, Mary, for you have found favor with God.

"Behold, you will conceive in your womb and bear a son, and you shall name him Jesus. He will be great and will be called Son of the Most High, and the Lord God will give him the throne of David his father, and he will rule over the house of Jacob forever, and of his kingdom there will be no end." But Mary said to the angel, "How can this be, since I have no relations with a man?" And the angel said to her in reply, "The Holy Spirit will come upon you, and the power of the Most High will overshadow you. Therefore the child to be born will be called holy, the Son of God. And behold, Elizabeth, your relative, has also conceived a son in her old age, and this is the sixth month for her who was called barren; for nothing will be impossible for God." Mary said, "Behold, I am the handmaid of the Lord. May it be done to me according to your word." Then the angel departed from her.

人

The announcement of the angel to Mary signals that the long-awaited time of the Messiah's coming is at hand. Centuries of watchful yearning culminates in the conception of Israel's Messiah in the womb of Mary. Though King David wanted to build a house for God out of stones and gold, Mary becomes a house that will build God's Messiah out of the cells and blood of her womb and with the nourishing milk of her breasts. Though Solomon, the son of David, eventually built a temple as the national sanctuary of his empire, Mary will give birth to the Savior of the whole world.

God desires to dwell with people in their ordinary dwellings and in their own human flesh. Those judged least likely by human standards are the most favored by God as instruments for revealing his covenant. God took the youthful shepherd David, the youngest and seemingly least qualified, to make him king. God took the young maiden Mary, a youthful woman making wedding plans in an insignificant little town in Galilee, to be the mother of the Messiah. Both accounts demonstrate the work of God's unmerited grace. It is not we who make dwelling places for God, but God who builds the house.

God's intervention in the world through Mary was unlike anything ever before in salvation history. Mary's virginal conception highlights the radical newness of God's action. God's unexpected grace was not a response to her yearning for a child, nor was it the result of anything she could have anticipated. God was doing an extraordinarily new thing in response to the watchful longing of his people. The child to be born would be the Messiah, the one who would be given the throne of David with an unending kingdom, and he would be the Son of God because he would be conceived through the overshadowing power of God's Spirit.

Mary's son would be a divine king. Unlike David, whose reign was bounded by the borders of time and Israel's empire, this king would fulfill all of history and embrace all of time, and "of his kingdom there will be no end" (Luke 1:33). But he would not come from splendid palaces, arrayed in royal robes and doing battle with enemies. He would come through Mary's womb, a hungry and crying child, the hope of the entire world. Without knowing how God would accomplish all of this, she accepts her mission with trust: "May it be done to me according to your word" (1:38). Mary opens a space for the divine presence to dwell within her, enabling God to make a new home within all of humankind.

MEDITATIO

⅄

Reflect on these Scriptures from the midst of your own desires and hopes. Consider God's promises to you and how God wishes to dwell with you.

- How does the portable ark of the covenant express Israel's inability to control and localize God? Why does God reject David's desire to build a temple? What do these indicators tell you about the God you worship?

- Why do human beings want to contain and control the boundless presence of God? In what ways do you try to define God's place in the world? In what ways do you put up obstacles to God's energizing presence in your life?

- How do these Scriptures demonstrate that God's salvation is undeserved and unearned by God's people? How do you experience salvation as God's unmerited grace?

- The angel's greeting to Mary, "Hail, full of grace! The Lord is with you" (Luke 1:28), indicates that he knew something about her that she did not know about herself. The divine grace working within her was a gift of God's love. Ponder these words as Mary did. What do they tell you about Mary as the model for Advent?

- In what areas of life do you need to hear these words of the angel: "Do not be afraid" (Luke 1:30) and "Nothing will be impossible for God" (1:37)?

ORATIO

Offer to God what you have discovered in yourself from your meditation. Begin your prayer with these words and then continue in your own words:

God of the covenant, you promised your king an eternal lineage and an everlasting reign, and you fulfilled your promises through the one who is Son of David and Son of Mary. Keep me watching in joyful hope for the completion of your promises and the coming of your kingdom.

When the words of prayer begin to seem inadequate and no longer necessary, move into the wordless prayer of contemplatio.

CONTEMPLATIO

God's covenant is eternal and his promises to you are unconditional. Spend some still moments resting with secure trust in God's everlasting faithfulness. You do not need to say or do anything. Simply accept the grace God wishes you to receive.

OPERATIO

How does the security of God's promises make a difference in the way you live your life? How can you grow in your confident trust in God when much of life seems increasingly less secure?

Chapter Five

Lectio Divina for Advent: Year C

First Sunday of Advent

LECTIO

Open your heart to the Spirit of God. Ask the Holy Spirit to lead you through this lectio divina, to guide your understanding, to kindle within you the fire of divine love.

Begin reading when you feel ready to hear God's voice speaking in Scripture. Slowly articulate the words so that you can listen better as you read.

JEREMIAH 33:14-16

The days are coming, says the LORD, when I will fulfill the promise I made to the house of Israel and Judah. In those days, in that time, I will raise up for David a just shoot; he shall do what is right and just in the land. In those days Judah shall be safe and Jerusalem shall dwell secure; this is what they shall call her: "The LORD our justice."

Although there is much in our culture at this time of year that invites us to take a nostalgic look backward—to childhood, to simpler times, to closer families—the season of Advent and its sacred texts encourage us to look forward. Advent is an invitation to hope, to trust in the future fulfillment of all God's promises. It is the season of joyful waiting and confident expectation.

The prophet Jeremiah saw that his people would be defeated by the Babylonians and that the Temple city of Jerusalem would be captured and destroyed. Nevertheless, in the midst of political chaos and despair, he remained a person of hope, and he communicates that hope to God's people: "The days are coming, says the Lord, when I will fulfill the promise I made" (33:14). He assures us that God keeps his promises to save us, forgive us, love us, and be with us now and forever.

Jeremiah was waiting and hoping for an ideal descendant of King David who might bring security and justice to God's people. This hope for a "just shoot" from David's branch, who would do "what is right and just" for God's people, is God's Messiah (33:15). Jeremiah sought to convince the people of his own day, and of our day as well, that their waiting and hoping would be fulfilled because God is trustworthy and keeps his promises.

After letting the words of Jeremiah fill you with hope, begin reading from the Gospel of Luke when you are ready. Let these words of Jesus strengthen within you the Advent virtues of patience, expectation, joy, and fidelity.

Luke 21:25-28, 34-36

Jesus said to his disciples: "There will be signs in the sun, the moon, and the stars, and on earth nations will be in dismay, perplexed by the roaring of the sea and the waves. People will die of fright in anticipation of what is coming upon the world, for the powers of the heavens will be shaken. And then they will see the Son of Man coming in a cloud with power and great glory. But when these signs begin to happen, stand erect and raise your heads because your redemption is at hand.

"Beware that your hearts do not become drowsy from carousing and drunkenness and the anxieties of daily life, and that day catch you by surprise like a trap. For that day will assault everyone who lives on the face of the earth. Be vigilant at all times and pray that you have the strength to escape the tribulations that are imminent and to stand before the Son of Man."

Advent reminds us that in the midst of our daily routine and plans, God has an eternal saving plan that is also in motion. This world, with its schedules, pursuits, and diversions, is gradually passing away. And much more swiftly, our own lives are passing away. The Scripture readings of this season urge us to watch and be vigilant.

Jesus teaches us how to live in the present moment, the time between his earthly ministry and his coming at the end of time. He warns us not to "become drowsy" (Luke 21:34) during the long wait. Like impassioned lovers whose fervor fades over time when their lives are lulled into routine, our love and devotion to Christ may grow dim. Jesus admonishes us not to become weighed down with the anxieties of daily life or to indulge in things that satisfy only for a time but do not last.

Luke's Gospel speaks of Christ's final advent and the signs and portents that will anticipate that majestic coming. Yet the days in which we live are always in some sense the last times, the days that are coming. Jesus teaches us that when things have gone from bad to worse, when our world seems to be literally falling apart, we can still trust in God's promises. While we remain watchful and vigilant, Jesus assures us that all will turn out well for those who remain faithful: "But when these signs begin to happen, stand erect and raise your heads because your redemption is at hand" (Luke 21:28). The final advent of the Lord is not to be feared but rather to be eagerly awaited. Be always watchful so as not to be taken by surprise, and prepare for the final and lasting embrace of the one who is love.

MEDITATIO

Spend some time reflecting on these two Scripture passages, which prepare God's people for both the first and the final coming of the Lord. In light of your own vigilance, seek the advice of these texts for your own preparation during Advent.

- Both Jeremiah and Jesus urge God's people to hope in the promises of God. In what ways have you experienced God fulfilling promises? What promises are you waiting for God to fulfill?

- All the Scriptures are about waiting with confident trust in God. How do you deal with waiting? What frustrates you most? What keeps you waiting?

- Jesus urges his disciples not to "become drowsy" (Luke 21:34). What makes people drowsy? How can you keep your heart from becoming drowsy this Advent?

- How do you feel when you think about the coming of Christ? Does it frighten you? Does it comfort you? How do the words of Jesus encourage you in light of his glorious return?

- Advent challenges us to look more to the future than to the past. What are the dangers of living in the past without an eye for the future? In what ways does living in light of God's future plans affect the way you live?

ORATIO

Jesus says, "Be vigilant at all times and pray that you have the strength to escape the tribulations that are imminent and to stand before the Son of Man" (Luke 21:36). With trusting faith, begin to pray in these words:

Coming Lord, your promises to us are wondrous and will fulfill the deepest longings of our hearts. Through your grace, keep me watchful and vigilant so that I will always be ready to experience the future you have in store for me.

Continue praying from your heart in the words God's Spirit gives you.

CONTEMPLATIO

Let the fire of God's love burn within your heart as you spend this time in wordless and vigilant silence. Trust that God is moving within you to make you ready for the future and to guide your way.

OPERATIO

If you knew that today was the great day of the Lord's coming, what would you do to prepare? Are these the things that you are doing or could be doing now? Choose one to focus on this week in order to prepare for the way of the Lord.

Second Sunday of Advent

LECTIO

Close off the day's distractions and enter into a quiet time with God's inspired word. Become aware of your breath as a gift of God, breathing in as you are filled with the presence of God and breathing out as you let go of all unnecessary anxiety.

Begin reading when you feel ready to hear God's voice in the sacred text.

BARUCH 5:1-9

Jerusalem, take off your robe of mourning and misery;
    put on the splendor of glory from God forever:
wrapped in the cloak of justice from God,
    bear on your head the mitre
    that displays the glory of the eternal name.
For God will show all the earth your splendor:
    you will be named by God forever
    the peace of justice, the glory of God's worship.

Up, Jerusalem! stand upon the heights;
    look to the east and see your children
gathered from the east and the west
    at the word of the Holy One,
    rejoicing that they are remembered by God.
Led away on foot by their enemies they left you:

but God will bring them back to you
borne aloft in glory as on royal thrones.
For God has commanded
that every lofty mountain be made low,
and that the age-old depths and gorges
be filled to level ground,
that Israel may advance secure in the glory of God.
The forests and every fragrant kind of tree
have overshadowed Israel at God's command;
for God is leading Israel in joy
by the light of his glory,
with his mercy and justice for company.

The much-neglected prophecies of Baruch are filled with long-ing and hope. The oppressed and scattered exiles in Babylon have turned away from their service of idols, wealth, and injustice, and have turned back to their service of the one God. Their repentance has opened the way for God's merciful rescue and their return to Jerusalem. Now, the once captive people take to the road, walk across the desert, and make their way back to their own land. The long and treacherous journey of the weary refugees is eased by the assurance that God is with them and that they are returning home to live in their covenant with God.

Meanwhile, Jerusalem waits. The devastated city, which has been mourning for her children who were forcibly taken away from her, now eagerly awaits their return. She is told to exchange her robe of mourning and misery for a splendid new mantle. Her new cloak is spun from justice and glory from God, and her priestly miter displays the eternal name of God. Her regal titles, "the peace of justice" and "the glory of God's worship" (Baruch 5:4) are displayed for all the earth to see. When Jerusalem knows the peace that comes with the practice of justice and when God is truly worshiped there, she will be a witness of God's glory to all the people of the world.

The response of mother Jerusalem is wonderfully envisioned as she is told to stand at the high point of the city and look eastward to see her rejoicing children streaming back home "at the word of the Holy One." If she despaired for her children, thinking God had forgotten them, the prophet insists that "they are remembered by God" (Baruch 5:5).

Their humiliating march into exile is reversed by their return "borne aloft in glory as on royal thrones" (Baruch 5:6). God has prepared the way by leveling the mountains and filling in the valleys, as if a monarch were returning to the imperial city. The desert has been transformed into a forest of fragrant trees for the enjoyment of the returning exiles. Grieving mother Jerusalem is blessed with the divine gift of joy as her children are led by God's light, with mercy and justice as their companions.

After listening to the words of God's prophet and being filled with renewed expectation, tend to the words of the Gospel according to Luke. Let the ministry of God's final prophet, John the Baptist, offer you hope, healing, restoration, and the chance for a new beginning.

LUKE 3:1-6

[handwritten: Roman World]

In the fifteenth year of the reign of Tiberius Caesar, when Pontius Pilate was governor of Judea, and Herod was tetrarch of Galilee, and his brother Philip tetrarch of the region of Ituraea and Trachonitis, and Lysanias was tetrarch of Abilene, during the high priesthood of Annas and Caiaphas, the word of God came to John the son of Zechariah in the desert. John went throughout the whole region of the Jordan, proclaiming a baptism of repentance for the forgiveness of sins, as it is written in the book of the words of the prophet Isaiah:

[handwritten margin left: Listened then Inspired]
[handwritten margin right: Repent]

> *A voice of one crying out in the desert:*
> *"Prepare the way of the Lord,*
>   *make straight his paths.*
> *Every valley shall be filled*
>   *and every mountain and hill shall be made low.*
> *The winding roads shall be made straight,*
>   *and the rough ways made smooth,*
> *and all flesh shall see the salvation of God."*

[handwritten: return of Exile = coming of Jesus; Smooth]
[handwritten: Jews & Gentiles]

Luke sets the stage for the ministry of John the Baptist in a way that connects the history of Israel with the sweep of the Roman Empire. The introduction of a list of Roman and Jewish officials in office—emperor, governor, tetrarchs, and high priests—indicates that God's salvation is located in human history, involving real persons in the context of real times and places. The list is also an indictment of the political powers and the religious establishment

[handwritten: ? not sure of indictment]

of the time. The word of God does not stop at palaces or at the Temple; rather, it came to John in the desert.

Luke's Gospel, like all the other Gospels, presents John the Baptist as the precursor of Jesus the Messiah. While extolling John's greatness, it insists that he is subordinate to Jesus, whose coming he proclaims. In anticipation of Jesus, John proclaims a baptism of repentance for the forgiveness of sins. Using the language of Isaiah, John's mission is to prepare the way for the coming of the Lord. Every obstacle must be eliminated. If the road is winding, it must be straightened. If it is rough, it must be smoothed. If a mountain is in the way, it must be leveled. If a valley hinders the travel, it must be filled in. These extravagant images express the critical importance and urgency of the Messiah's coming and the necessity of preparation.

Unlike the other Evangelists, Luke highlights the universal significance of Jesus by expanding the quotation from the prophet Isaiah with the final line, "and all flesh shall see the salvation of God" (3:6). The salvation to be offered in Jesus Christ extends to the whole world. In him God's salvation will extend, not just to Jerusalem, but throughout Galilee and Judea and even to the full extent of the Roman Empire.

MEDITATIO

God brought his people through the desert on their way home to Jerusalem and called John to prepare the way for Christ in the desert. In the quiet and stillness of your own heart, ponder these Scripture passages in relation to your developing life in Christ.

- In your imagination, let yourself envision the refugees streaming back to Jerusalem, "rejoicing that they are remembered by God" (Baruch 5:5). What do you see with the eyes of faith? What do you hear with the ear of your heart? What are some of the emotions you feel within yourself?

[handwritten margin note: HAPPY & PRAYER]

- Why was Israel's return from exile in the sixth century B.C. a source of hope for early Christians? Why should it be a source of hope for you today? *From Nothing to Hope for Something*

[handwritten margin note: Repentance Needed]

- Both Baruch and Luke know that <u>repentance and conver</u>sion are necessary before the experience of God's intervention in history. Why is this turning away from false worship and injustice so necessary for our experience of freedom and salvation? *Stop digging the hole*

[handwritten margin note: Does God work thru "the enemies" or "sheep"]

- Why did God not send his word to the palaces of political rulers or to the Temple of the religious establishment but to John in the desert? <u>What does God's targeted audience say about the ways that God works in the world today?</u> *Great question*

- How do the prophetic words "and <u>all flesh shall see the</u> salvation of God" (Luke 3:6) offer you hope this Advent? What is so important about the universality of God's salvation? *OT concentrates on Jews + is prejudice agst Arabs   Ishmael Esau   NT (Jesus) brings all together*

ORATIO

Prayer begins by listening to God's word with a receptive mind, followed by meditation on that word with the understanding of the heart. When you are ready to respond to God's word with the words of your own prayer, you might begin in this way:

Light to the nations, you free your people from exile and guide them on the way that leads to your presence. Help me prepare a straight path for your coming by letting the good news of Christ's coming open and fill my heart.

Continue your prayer, asking God to help you to trust him completely.

CONTEMPLATIO

In the quiet stillness of the desert within you, imagine God leading you to his divine presence. Allow God to work within you, preparing you in whatever way you need.

OPERATIO

What are the mountains, valleys, winding roads, and rough ways that impede your preparation for the Lord this Advent? What action could you take this week to make the coming of the Lord more straight and smooth?

Third Sunday of Advent

LECTIO

Light the rose-colored third candle of Advent or place some other image before you to focus your attention. Remove from your mind and heart whatever hinders you from receiving God's word.

When you are ready to listen, vocalize the words of the text so that you not only read with your eyes but hear with your ears.

ZEPHANIAH 3:14-18A

Shout for joy, O daughter Zion!
   Sing joyfully, O Israel!
Be glad and exult with all your heart,
   O daughter Jerusalem!
The LORD has removed the judgment against you,
   he has turned away your enemies;
the King of Israel, the LORD, is in your midst,
   you have no further misfortune to fear.
On that day, it shall be said to Jerusalem:
   Fear not, O Zion, be not discouraged!
The LORD, your God, is in your midst,
   a mighty savior;
he will rejoice over you with gladness,
   and renew you in his love,

[handwritten margin notes: Exult with all your heart; RELAX (forgiven); FEAR NOT; God REJOICES; RENEWED LOVE]

113

he will sing joyfully because of you,   *God sings out*
    as one sings at festivals.

⋏

The prophet Zephaniah demonstrates Israel's relationship with God as a movement from rebellion to restoration to rejoicing. At the end of his writings, the prophet expresses the joyful shouting and singing that took place at the religious festivals of ancient Israel and uses it as an image to describe the happiness that God's people will experience as they are gathered once more in Jerusalem. This joyful noise expresses the gladness and exultation that fills their hearts because God has removed judgment against them and turned away their enemies. They have no reason to fear further misfortune because God is in their midst.

The joy that concludes the prophecy is almost unimaginable. Not only do God's people rejoice over their forgiveness and salvation, but God also rejoices and sings with them. God expresses absolute delight in renewing his people in love. It is a mutual gladness that wants to be shared in wider and wider circles.

As you let the joy of God's salvation fill your heart, turn to the fullest expression of saving joy in Luke's Gospel. The good news of Jesus Christ is God's expression of delight in his creation.

LUKE 3:10-18

The crowds asked John the Baptist, "What should we do?" He said to them in reply, "Whoever has two cloaks should share with the person who has none. And whoever has food should do likewise." Even tax collectors came to be baptized

Share stuff

No bullying *No cheating*

and they said to him, "Teacher, what should we do?" He answered them, "Stop collecting more than what is prescribed." Soldiers also asked him, "And what is it that we should do?" He told them, "Do not practice extortion, do not falsely accuse anyone, and be satisfied with your wages."

Now the people were filled with expectation, and all were asking in their hearts whether John might be the Christ. John answered them all, saying, "I am baptizing you with water, *Water* but one mightier than I is coming. I am not worthy to loosen *vs* the thongs of his sandals. He will baptize you with the Holy *Holy* Spirit and fire. His winnowing fan is in his hand to clear his *Spirit* threshing floor and to gather the wheat into his barn, but the chaff he will burn with unquenchable fire." Exhorting them in many other ways, he preached good news to the people.

After people have responded to John's invitation to repent, he urges them to produce good fruit as evidence of their repentance. Their transformed hearts are not just matters of interior illumination but of changed lifestyles. Repentance involves an intellectual realization in the mind, a motivational change of the will, and a concrete alteration of behavior. So one by one, the people ask John the Baptist, "What should we do?" (Luke 3:10).

John's responses are tailored to each person according to his or her circumstances. His advice feels a bit too specific for comfort: "Whoever has two cloaks should share with the person who has none. And whoever has food should do likewise" (Luke 3:11). After all, most of us have more than one coat and plenty of food in the freezer. Imagine what could happen if, adding a few more examples, those of us who have two cars would give one to a poor family who needs it to get a job. Or what if those who own a vacation home would find a homeless family to live there? John's examples seem to touch on the specific excesses of each person. We might imagine ourselves turning clothes out of our closets, furniture out of our homes, and valuables from our lockboxes. Such actions might give us a greater sense of peace and simplicity. Then, according to John the Baptist, we would be ready for the coming of the Lord.

John seems to associate Advent preparedness with generosity toward other people who are in need. The implication is that if we don't feel ready for the day of the Lord, it may be because we are too busy defending our possessions, our power, and our privilege. The one who is coming, who baptizes with the Holy Spirit and fire, is here with his winnowing fan to separate the wheat from the chaff of our lives. We might conclude from John's words that the Holy Spirit and fire mean judgment and destruction. But in Jesus, the Holy Spirit provides the spiritual energy to share with others and not oppress them, and the fire provides the passion to persevere. The Holy Spirit will blow through our lives to separate the wheat and the chaff, preserving the wheat for God's kingdom, and the fire will burn up the useless chaff of selfishness and sin.

The Gospel tells us that whether we are a tax collector, a soldier, a butcher, or a baker, when we are living under the good news of God's reign, our lives and what we do with them matter. As we are refined in the fire of God's Spirit, all that keeps us from experiencing God's delight and true joy will be burned away. Then God will rejoice over us with gladness, renew us in his love, and sing joyfully with us as one sings at festivals (Zephaniah 3:17-18).

MEDITATIO

Allow the power of God's word to work within you. Let it call you to repentance, and let it renew your life from the inside out.

- Zephaniah expresses the joy of God's people gathered back in Jerusalem. When have you been the happiest? What gives you the greatest lasting joy? *Having Harden Kids' success*

- The crowds asked John the Baptist, "What should we do?" (Luke 3:10). Considering the responses of John addressed to people in different situations, which advice seems best for you? *Share stuff*

- Making a choice would be easier if someone else could tell us which option is the right one. But no one can answer that question for us. When have you had to make a life-changing decision? Did you receive any confirmation that you made the right choice? *leaving seminary!! proposing to Karen birth of Kristin Yes,*

- How does the understanding of the action of "the Holy Spirit and fire" conveyed by John the Baptist (Luke 3:16) differ from the way God works through the ministry of Jesus? Do John's words fill you with fear or hope? *Hope*

- Deep and lasting joy is a sure sign of the presence of the Holy Spirit. What is the source of your rose-colored joy as you look to this Gaudete Sunday?

117

ORATIO

⋏

Respond to God's word in these Scriptures with repentance and a renewed heart. Begin with these words:

Mighty Savior, you rejoice over me with gladness and renew me in your love. Send your Holy Spirit to refine my heart and burn away the chaff of frivolous and selfish desires. Produce within my life the good fruits of genuine repentance.

Continue praying with a repentant heart and a deep desire for God.

CONTEMPLATIO

⋏

The prophet says that God "will rejoice over you with gladness, / and renew you in his love, / he will sing joyfully because of you, / as one sings at festivals" (Zephaniah 3:17-18). Imagine God rejoicing over you and singing because of you. Rest in God's presence and let him transform your heart.

OPERATIO

⋏

"What should we do?" the people ask John the Baptist (Luke 3:10). There is no one-size-fits-all response. Ask the Holy Spirit what you should do this week in order to produce the good fruits of repentance and to prepare for the Lord's coming.

Fourth Sunday of Advent

LECTIO

In a comfortable and quiet place of prayer, light the fourth candle of the Advent wreath. Become aware of the rhythms of your breathing. Ask God's Spirit to fill your heart and guide your listening.

MICAH 5:1-4A

Thus says the LORD:
You, Bethlehem-Ephrathah,
    too small to be among the clans of Judah,
from you shall come forth for me
    one who is to be ruler in Israel;
whose origin is from of old,
    from ancient times.
Therefore the Lord will give them up, until the time
    when she who is to give birth has borne,
and the rest of his kindred shall return
    to the children of Israel.
He shall stand firm and shepherd his flock
    by the strength of the LORD,
    in the majestic name of the LORD, his God;
and they shall remain, for now his greatness

shall reach to the ends of the earth;
he shall be peace.

人

The prophet Micah was a contemporary of Isaiah. He, too, spoke God's word about a coming savior from the line of King David. Like Isaiah, who prophesied of a young maiden who would give birth to a king known as "Emmanuel" (7:14), Micah foretells that a royal woman will give birth to the king in Bethlehem. Like his ancestor David, the shepherd king, this coming ruler will shepherd his flock and bring security to his people. The reign of this great king will extend "to the ends of the earth" (Micah 5:3), and his rule will be characterized by peace.

Bethlehem became well-known in Israel's history because it was the home of Jesse, the father of David, and the birthplace of Israel's greatest king. The double designation "Bethlehem-Ephrathah" (Micah 5:1) refers to the clan of people who live in the area of Bethlehem. The prophecy that the coming messianic ruler will come from Bethlehem implies that he will be a new David, coming to fulfill all the promises God made through King David of old.

Micah describes Bethlehem-Ephrathah as "too small to be among the clans of Judah" (5:1). Throughout biblical history, God has been doing wondrous things with small and unlikely people and places that we would not expect. Of course, the gospel confirms that Jesus fulfills all the great prophecies given for the house of David. The announcement that the Messiah and Savior of the world will be conceived by the young maiden of Nazareth and be given birth in a manger in Bethlehem is the fullest expression of this biblical theme that God's saving power is manifested in small, unlikely, and unexpected ways.

LUKE 1:39-45

Mary set out and traveled to the hill country in haste to a town of Judah, where she entered the house of Zechariah and greeted Elizabeth. When Elizabeth heard Mary's greeting, the infant leaped in her womb, and Elizabeth, filled with the Holy Spirit, cried out in a loud voice and said, "Blessed are you among women, and blessed is the fruit of your womb. And how does this happen to me, that the mother of my Lord should come to me? For at the moment the sound of your greeting reached my ears, the infant in my womb leaped for joy. Blessed are you who believed that what was spoken to you by the Lord would be fulfilled."

Mary, the teenage maiden, travels quickly to the house of her elderly cousin, Elizabeth. Somewhere in the hill country of Judah, the two women meet with babies in their wombs. In these two unknown women, bearing their tiny yet-to-be-born children, embracing each other in a most unlikely place, the dawn of salvation is about to unfold. Truly, God's saving power is manifested in small, unlikely, and unexpected ways.

Elizabeth is the wise mentor, who offers her young relative the strength of experience. Mary is the generous novice, desiring to help Elizabeth cope with a difficult pregnancy. These two women represent the meeting of the old covenant and the new. The elder one will have a son who will be the last great figure of ancient Israel; the younger will have a son who will usher in the new age of salvation. In Mary, the new covenant reaches out to the old, affirming its crucial significance in God's plan and preparing for its culmination. In Elizabeth, the old covenant recognizes its own fulfillment and honors the coming of the new. The joyful unity of these two women expresses the harmony between the traditional faith of Israel and the coming of the Savior, a completion and a new beginning of God's saving work in the world.

Elizabeth proclaims that Mary is most blessed for two reasons. First, she is blessed because she bears the Lord in her womb: "Blessed are you among women, and blessed is the fruit of your womb" (Luke 1:42). Second, she is blessed because she has believed the word of God: "Blessed are you who believed that what was spoken to you by the Lord would be fulfilled" (1:45). Thus, Mary is praised both as the mother of the Lord and as a model for Christian believers.

MEDITATIO

Read these two texts again, pausing to reflect each time that a phrase speaks directly to you. Place yourself in the situation of Mary and Elizabeth, and consider how you respond to the ways God is working within you.

- What are some ways that Micah indicates that God's saving power is manifested in small, unlikely, and unexpected ways? What are other indicators that God works in the world and in individual lives in these ways?

- Both Micah and the Gospel of Luke suggest that we must be ready for the surprising ways that God's redeeming power breaks through in unexpected places. What are some ways that you have been surprised by God? When have you encountered God's mercy in an unexpected way?

- What is your usual response to adolescents, the elderly, the unborn, and the poor? What does it mean that the world's salvation unfolds through them?

- God's timing is difficult for both Elizabeth and Mary. It would have been easier if Elizabeth had given birth to her child at an earlier age. It would have been easier if Mary had conceived her child after her marriage to Joseph. How do these women help you accept the many difficulties that come with saying yes to God?

- Mary is the ideal disciple because she is committed to God's word. After receiving the good news, she hastens to share that word with another in need. She surrenders herself to God's plan, she is full of gratitude for the gifts she receives, and she has a contemplative sense of wonder at the mysteries of God. What virtues of Mary do you want to imitate during this season?

ORATIO

After listening to God through your reading and reflection, respond to God through the words of your prayer. You may wish to begin with these words:

Son of God and Son of Mary, you came to the world through the will and the womb of a young virgin. Prepare my heart to receive your redeeming love as I prepare to remember your birth in Bethlehem.

Continue expressing your heart to the Lord, who knows you intimately, cares about you deeply, and accepts you unconditionally.

CONTEMPLATIO

Place your memories and your imagination in the heart of Mary and consider the love she has for her divine Son. Let God's love surround and embrace you and fill you with a love like that of Mary.

OPERATIO

The visit of Mary and Elizabeth calls us to honor the young, the elderly, the poor, and the powerless. What could you do this week to offer respect for these "little ones" as you prepare your heart to celebrate the wonder of the Incarnation?

Chapter Six

Lectio Divina for Christmas and Epiphany: Years A, B, and C

Christmas Mass during the Night

LECTIO

Light a Christmas candle or sit before a nativity scene to keep you focused on the saving event of Christ's birth.

Read these familiar texts as if for the first time. Listen to them in a new way, guided by God's renewing Spirit.

ISAIAH 9:1-6

The people who walked in darkness
   have seen a great light;
upon those who dwelt in the land of gloom
   a light has shone.
You have brought them abundant joy
   and great rejoicing,
as they rejoice before you as at the harvest,
   as people make merry when dividing spoils.
For the yoke that burdened them,
   the pole on their shoulder,
and the rod of their taskmaster
   you have smashed, as on the day of Midian.
For every boot that tramped in battle,
   every cloak rolled in blood,

will be burned as fuel for flames.
For a child is born to us, a son is given us;
    upon his shoulder dominion rests.
They name him Wonder-Counselor, God-Hero,
    Father-Forever, Prince of Peace.
His dominion is vast
    and forever peaceful,
from David's throne, and over his kingdom,
    which he confirms and sustains
by judgment and justice,
    both now and forever.
The zeal of the LORD of hosts will do this!

In a time of darkness and gloom for the people of Israel, when their land was being conquered and destroyed, Isaiah's prophecy shone with brilliant hope. The ancient prophet proclaims that God will rescue his people from their subjugation—the yoke, the pole, the rod of their oppressors. Their accoutrements of war will be burned as fuel for the flames. The deliverance of God's people will be like a great light shining forth, a time of rejoicing upon the darkness and gloom of the land.

This light and joy will be brought to Israel through the birth of a child who will be king. This royal child is given titles that seem almost divine. "Wonder-Counselor" designates one who devises wise plans and is able to carry them out. "God-Hero" designates a king who shares in the power of God to do whatever is necessary for the salvation of his people. "Father-Forever" stresses the king's faithful, devoted care of his people. "Prince of Peace" expresses the peacemaking qualities of this king, who will usher the kingdom under his rule into a state of harmony and completeness (Isaiah 9:5).

Partial fulfillment of Isaiah's prophecy occurred in Isaiah's lifetime, through successful battles and kings who brought religious reforms. But the wonderful era expressed by the prophet was projected into a more distant future. This messianic age would be a time in which a king of David's line would secure the kingdom in a way different from war and political alliances. The coming reign of peace would mean judgment of the violent ways of the world and justice for the oppressed. With the advent of each new king, the people's hopes flamed anew.

The anticipated Messiah would be an ideal king and savior. Under his reign, the kingdom of David would be vast and forever peaceful. Since God does not abandon his people and always keeps his promises, the birth of the Messiah changed this dream of Isaiah into a reality for the world. We cannot enter this kingdom with swords, hatred, despair, or gloomy hearts. Only those who "have seen a great light" can enter this kingdom of God and his Son, the Messiah (Isaiah 9:1).

LUKE 2:1-14

In those days a decree went out from Caesar Augustus that the whole world should be enrolled. This was the first enrollment, when Quirinius was governor of Syria. So all went to be enrolled, each to his own town. And Joseph too went up from Galilee from the town of Nazareth to Judea, to the city of David that is called Bethlehem, because he was of the house and family of David, to be enrolled with Mary, his betrothed, who was with child. While they were there, the time came for her to have her child, and she gave birth to her firstborn son. She wrapped him in swaddling clothes and laid him in a manger, because there was no room for them in the inn.

Now there were shepherds in that region living in the fields and keeping the night watch over their flock. The angel of the Lord appeared to them and the glory of the Lord shone around them, and they were struck with great fear. The angel said to them, "Do not be afraid; for behold, I proclaim to you good news of great joy that will be for all the people. For today in the city of David a savior has been born for you who is Christ and Lord. And this will be a sign for you: you will find an infant wrapped in swaddling clothes and lying in a manger." And suddenly there was a multitude of the heavenly host with the angel, praising God and saying:

"Glory to God in the highest
and on earth peace to those on whom his favor rests."

Listening to the birth narrative of Luke's Gospel, we are struck by the contrasts between the infant born of Mary and the messianic child of whom Isaiah speaks (9:5). The "Wonder-Counselor" is given birth in the tiny village of Bethlehem. The "God-Hero" is wrapped in swaddling clothes and laid in a manger. The glorious news of the "Father-Forever" is announced to simple shepherds in the fields. The "Prince of Peace" is born into a people living under the heel of Roman occupation.

Though Luke's narrative may seem placid and charming because we know it so well, beneath the surface we glimpse its harsh political and social realities. An imperial decree requires a census of all the people subject to the Roman Empire. While the entire world is on the move, an obscure couple makes their way toward their ancestral village of Bethlehem. With her child playfully kicking beneath her ribs, Mary quietly endures backaches and leg cramps during their long journey from Nazareth. During the unpredictable winter season of Palestine, Mary and Joseph sometimes feel the grit of sand blowing against their faces, and at other times they are drenched with rain. Because there is no room in the usual lodging places, the child is born in a stable. And after being wrapped in bands of cloth, the traditional practice that kept a child warm and protected, he is laid in a manger, a feeding trough from which the animals ate.

Luke portrays the birth of Jesus as the meeting of heaven and earth. In the birth of Jesus, Israel's hopes for the Messiah from David's line are fulfilled. Through the new heart beating against Mary's breast, the world will be transformed. But Caesar Augustus can't see it even though he rules over the whole known world. The innkeepers in Bethlehem don't know it because they turn him away. Only the humble, shabby shepherds learn the significance of his birth. They are stunned by divine glory and struck with fear. Yet to them is communicated "good news of great joy" for all people (Luke 2:10), tidings that will be sung down through the ages in gratitude for this night.

The angel's announcement is the message of the entire gospel: the newborn of Bethlehem is Savior, Christ, and Lord. As Savior, Jesus liberates people from sin and heals the divisions that separate people from God. As Christ, Jesus is the anointed heir of David who will establish God's kingdom. As Lord, Jesus is the transcendent One who carries divine authority. The angels give glory to God who reigns in heaven, and they evoke peace for the people of the earth. A baby wrapped in cloth and lying in a feeding trough is not the kind of "sign" (Luke 2:12) one might expect at the birth of the Savior, Christ, and Lord. Both his simple poverty and his glorious sovereignty invite us to ponder the mystery of this humble Savior who will call the lowly to himself. Because he did not choose wealth and power, we can come to him in rags, unembarrassed. Because he became like us, we can become like him.

MEDITATIO

Ponder these glorious Scriptures of Christmas with a view toward the new life born into the world. Like the shepherd, you are summoned by God's word to ponder the sign and to know that Jesus is Savior, Christ, and Lord.

- What heavy yokes have you experienced? In what way has God "smashed" (Isaiah 9:3) one of your yokes?

- Imagine yourself in Bethlehem on the night of Christ's birth. What do you see and hear? What emotions do you feel? How do you react?

- Of all the people of the world that the angels could have visited, why would God want the Savior's birth first announced to shepherds? How might you want to imitate their response?

- What tasks and pursuits cause you to forget how much God loves those who are weak and vulnerable? How do you forget that you are also weak and vulnerable?

- What does the "sign" given to the shepherds in Bethlehem (Luke 2:2) teach you about our Savior? How does the manner in which God chose to save us make a difference in your life?

ORATIO

After you've listened to what God has to say to you through these Scripture passages, consider what you want to say to God in response. You might want to begin with these words:

Savior, Christ, and Lord, you were presented to the world in a lowly manger and announced to humble shepherds. As I contemplate the mystery of your simple birth, help me be a humble herald of this "good news of great joy" (Luke 2:10).

Continue responding to God in prayer in the words that arise from your own experience with the Scriptures.

CONTEMPLATIO

When the words of prayer are no longer necessary or helpful, just rest silently in God's presence. Reflect on the mystery of God's incomprehensible love in your life.

OPERATIO

As we celebrate the joy of Christmas, remember those who are oppressed by poverty, violence, and tragedy, either locally or globally. Choose to do something this week to help children who are victims of these harsh and oppressive situations.

Christmas Mass during the Day

LECTIO

As you prepare for your attentive listening to God's word, kiss the words of the sacred texts as an expression of your devotion. Ask the Holy Spirit to help you listen and respond to the sacra pagina as you reflect on the texts for Christmas Day.

When you have quieted your external and internal distractions, dedicate this time for sacred conversation with God.

ISAIAH 52:7-10

How beautiful upon the mountains
    are the feet of him who brings glad tidings,
announcing peace, bearing good news,
    announcing salvation, and saying to Zion,
    "Your God is King!"

Hark! Your sentinels raise a cry,
    together they shout for joy,
for they see directly, before their eyes,
    the LORD restoring Zion.
Break out together in song,
    O ruins of Jerusalem!
For the LORD comforts his people,

he redeems Jerusalem.
The LORD has bared his holy arm
in the sight of all the nations;
all the ends of the earth will behold
the salvation of our God.

Christmas is filled with glad tidings and the joyful sound of carols proclaiming the Messiah's coming. On this day the prophet directs our listening to a chorus of voices singing the good news of our divine king. The first voice is the messenger running to Jerusalem to convey the news of God's victory. As the courier is about to complete his journey, he appears over the crest of the mountains that surround Jerusalem. His feet are bruised and torn after the long run, yet of those feet the prophet exclaims, "How beautiful!" These are the feet that bring the good news of peace and salvation (Isaiah 52:7).

The sentinels standing watch upon the walls of Jerusalem are the first to see the approaching runner and to hear his message. They take up the joyful song and join the chorus because they understand at once that the good news means that the Lord is restoring Zion. Finally, even the ruins of Jerusalem are summoned to join in the chorus and to sing for joy. For God is comforting his people and redeeming Jerusalem.

This event—God's victory opening the way for his people's return to Jerusalem—is described in global proportions. "All the nations" witness God's salvation, a victory that affects "all the ends of the earth" (Isaiah 7:10). God's restoration of his people gives hope to all people in bondage. It gives orientation to those who feel lost and renewal to those who experience the crushing sadness of grief. For all defeated and disillusioned people everywhere, this chorus of messenger, sentinels, and restored Jerusalem is a Christmas carol filled with hope and confidence.

This song of praise for God's redeeming power ends the time of exile and introduces the gospel of Jesus Christ. After savoring this carol of salvation, begin listening to the hymn that introduces the Gospel according to John.

JOHN 1:1-18

In the beginning was the Word,
   and the Word was with God,
   and the Word was God.
He was in the beginning with God.
All things came to be through him,
   and without him nothing came to be.
What came to be through him was life,
   and this life was the light of the human race;
the light shines in the darkness,
   and the darkness has not overcome it.
A man named John was sent from God. He came for testimony, to testify to the light, so that all might believe through him. He was not the light, but came to testify to the light. The true light, which enlightens everyone, was coming into the world.

He was in the world,
> and the world came to be through him,
> but the world did not know him.

He came to what was his own,
> but his own people did not accept him.

But to those who did accept him he gave power to become children of God, to those who believe in his name, who were born not by natural generation nor by human choice nor by a man's decision but of God.

And the Word became flesh
> and made his dwelling among us,
> and we saw his glory,
> the glory as of the Father's only Son,
> full of grace and truth.

John testified to him and cried out, saying, "This was he of whom I said, 'The one who is coming after me ranks ahead of me because he existed before me.'" From his fullness we have all received, grace in place of grace, because while the law was given through Moses, grace and truth came through Jesus Christ. No one has ever seen God. The only Son, God, who is at the Father's side, has revealed him.

This prologue to John's Gospel has been the Gospel reading for Christmas Day from the Church's early centuries. Here there is neither angel nor manger, neither shepherds nor virgin mother. For John, the story of Jesus' birth begins long before Bethlehem in the realm of God's timeless eternity. Before the ages, "the Word was with God, / and the Word was God" (1:1). The Word, we might say, is God's self-expression, his reaching out, revealing the divine nature and sharing the divine life.

The first expression of God's word was creation itself. Throughout history God spoke the divine word through the Torah and the prophets. Finally, this divine communication culminated in the fullest and ultimate Word, Jesus Christ himself. The eternal Word has been born into frail humanity: "The Word became flesh and made his dwelling among us" (John 1:14). The mission of Jesus, the Word, is to reveal to us the hidden nature of God—to show us by his life that God is loving, generous, merciful, and forgiving—and to share God's life with us. The incarnate Word gives to humanity the power to become children of God, to be reborn, not of natural descent or human initiative, but through the grace of God. As God's own children, we are able to grow increasingly secure in our divine parent's love for us.

The Word of God is "the light of the human race," "the true light, which enlightens everyone" (John 1:4, 9). The motif of light and darkness is prevalent throughout John's Gospel, describing the presence of Christ in the midst of earth's shadows and the darkness of sin, ignorance, and death. The glory of God is displayed for all to see in Jesus Christ, the light that shines triumphantly in a darkened world. He is the fullness of all the "grace and truth" that God gave to Israel in the past, and "from his fullness we have all received, grace in place of grace" (John 1:14, 16). Although grace was indeed given through Moses and the Torah, the fullness of grace, the ultimate grace, is given through Jesus Christ.

MEDITATIO

︿

God has sung these inspired words to the world through their inspired authors. Seek to assimilate these texts in all their depth so that you can respond to them with your life.

- What can you learn from these words of Isaiah about being a messenger of the gospel to others? In what way are your "feet" (52:7) engaged in the service of God's reign? How can you evangelize the people around you?

- The Christmas story in John's Gospel is radically different from the accounts in the Gospels of Matthew and Luke. Why did John choose to begin his Gospel "in the beginning" (1:1) rather than with the earthly conception and birth of Jesus?

- In what sense can we say that the Word is God's self-revelation? Is God a person of his word? How are your words the extension of yourself to others? Are you a person of your word?

- John's prologue makes it clear that the Word did not become manifest merely as an apparition, but truly "became flesh and made his dwelling among us" (1:14). What difference does this divine "enfleshment" mean for your life?

- In what ways is Jesus Christ the true light that brightens the darkness of your life this Christmas? How can you let his light shine more brightly in your heart and in the world around you?

ORATIO

After reflecting on the meaning of these Christmas texts, respond to God in prayer:

Word of God, you shine in the world and enlighten my life. Cast out the darkness of falsehood and ignorance. Show me the truth, love, and goodness of God. Open my heart to your grace.

Pray in praise of the Incarnation, in petition for the grace to believe in Christ, in repentance for promoting the darkness, or in thanksgiving for the insights you have received from God's word.

CONTEMPLATIO

The Son of God responded to the waiting world with his remarkable condescension to assume human life. He became like us so that we could become like him. Ask him to shine the light of his grace and truth into your life today.

OPERATIO

Resolve to actively participate in the Mass of Christmas. Listen carefully to the words of the liturgy, involve yourself in the music, gestures, and actions of the service, and allow the grace of the Eucharist to gradually transform your life. Prepare for the coming of Christ to you in the Eucharist.

The Epiphany of the Lord

LECTIO

The feast of Epiphany celebrates the manifestation of Christ to the world. For Jew and Gentile alike, God's love bursts forth like a light that pierces the darkness. Light a candle or sit in the presence of the manger scene approached by the three Magi bearing gifts.

When you are prepared, read these texts aloud, reading with your eyes and lips and listening with your ears and your heart. Hear these inspired words in a new way, guided by the light of God's renewing Spirit.

ISAIAH 60:1-6

Rise up in splendor, Jerusalem! Your light has come,
    the glory of the Lord shines upon you.
See, darkness covers the earth,
    and thick clouds cover the peoples;
but upon you the LORD shines,
    and over you appears his glory.
Nations shall walk by your light,
    and kings by your shining radiance.
Raise your eyes and look about;
    they all gather and come to you:
your sons come from afar,
    and your daughters in the arms of their nurses.

Then you shall be radiant at what you see,
    your heart shall throb and overflow,
for the riches of the sea shall be emptied out before you,
    the wealth of nations shall be brought to you.
Caravans of camels shall fill you,
    dromedaries from Midian and Ephah;
all from Sheba shall come
    bearing gold and frankincense,
    and proclaiming the praises of the LORD.

⋏

The contrast of darkness and light is a timeless image that runs throughout the Scriptures. In the darkness people lose their way, and the cover of darkness suggests intrigue and deception. In their vulnerability and fright, people instinctively seek the light. Studies have shown that we need darkness to sleep, but we need light to thrive. With light we can find our way, feel secure, and perceive rightly. The Christmas season itself is a feast of lights, with candles glowing in the darkness and sparkling luminaries brightening our homes. Our lives are aglow with the bonds of love, family, and friendship remembered and strengthened.

Isaiah uses the metaphor of darkness to speak of the gloomy plight of Israel in exile and of light to refer to the hope of future restoration. Here the prophet proclaims that the darkness of despair has been lifted and a new day has dawned for God's people. The light of God's glory shining on Jerusalem will so transform God's people that the light will shine forth to the other nations. In fact, all the nations of the world will walk by that light, will acknowledge and enjoy that light, and so will proclaim the praises of the God of Israel.

The prophet envisions a great procession to the holy city. First will come the dispersed sons and daughters of Israel, who will then be followed by people from many nations bringing gifts by camel caravans to proclaim the glory of God. Mention of the retinue from Sheba is reminiscent of the visit of the Queen of Sheba to King Solomon (1 Kings 10:1-2). From her distant land, she visited the son of David, presenting him with gifts of gold, spices, and precious stones.

The Gospel passage from Matthew shows that Isaiah's "light to the nations" (cf. 42:6; 49:6; cf. 60:3) is truly the Savior of the world. Both Isaiah and the Magi from the East point to the universality of God's salvation offered by Christ. His Incarnation illumines us all so that through us, God can illumine the whole world

MATTHEW 2:1-12

When Jesus was born in Bethlehem of Judea, in the days of King Herod, behold, magi from the east arrived in Jerusalem, saying, "Where is the newborn king of the Jews? We saw his star at its rising and have come to do him homage." When King Herod heard this, he was greatly troubled, and all Jerusalem with him. Assembling all the chief priests and the scribes of the people, he inquired of them where the Christ was to be born. They said to him, "In Bethlehem of Judea, for thus it has been written through the prophet:

And you, Bethlehem, land of Judah,
   are by no means least among the rulers of Judah;
since from you shall come a ruler,
   who is to shepherd my people Israel."

Then Herod called the magi secretly and ascertained from them the time of the star's appearance. He sent them to Bethlehem and said, "Go and search diligently for the child. When you have found him, bring me word, that I too may go and do him homage." After their audience with the king they set out. And behold, the star that they had seen at its rising preceded them, until it came and stopped over the place where the child was. They were overjoyed at seeing the star, and on entering the house they saw the child with Mary his mother. They prostrated themselves and did him homage. Then they opened their treasures and offered him gifts of gold, frankincense, and myrrh. And having been warned in a dream not to return to Herod, they departed for their country by another way.

The paranoia, deceit, and secrecy of King Herod express the darkness that lay over the land of Judea. Known for his murderous cruelty, Herod was insanely jealous of any perceived threats to his power. So when news reaches him that a child has been born who is destined to be king, conflict is inevitable. But a shining star brings light into this darkness. In the ancient days of Moses, a seer from the East named Balaam blessed Israel's future by proclaiming a coming king who would be announced by a star: "A star shall advance from Jacob, and a scepter shall rise from Israel" (Numbers 24:17). As the Magi come from the East, the star precedes them and stops over the place where Jesus has been born.

The Magi are avid scholars of spiritual mysteries. Whether these seekers are Persian priests, Babylonian astronomers, Nabataean spice traders, or wise seekers from other places to the East, their significance lies in that they are Gentiles from distant nations. Later, tradition embellished the biblical account by giving names and royal titles to these Magi: Melchior, king of Persia; Gaspar, king of India; and Balthasar, king of Arabia. The wise men interpret the star as a divine sign pointing to the Messiah and seek to find him: "Where is the newborn king of the Jews? We saw his star at its rising and have come to do him homage" (Matthew 2:2).

Matthew's Gospel sets up a stark contrast between the dark fear of Herod and the adoring homage of the Magi. While Herod plots the death of the child, the strangers from the East kneel before him and offer him gifts worthy of a king. These Gentile Magi who come to worship Christ anticipate all the believers from all the nations who will be called to salvation through this King from the line of David. His origin in Bethlehem points to his destiny. Some will accept him and offer him worship; others will reject him and seek to put him to death. The disciples of Jesus will meet a similar reception when they proclaim the gospel after the resurrection. Some people will accept the saving good news; others will oppose it and violently persecute the community of faith. From his birth, Jesus is destined to be the suffering Messiah whose worldwide dominion will bring salvation to all the nations.

MEDITATIO

Λ

Consider the new insights and transformed way of life you could experience from truly listening to these Scripture passages and taking them to heart.

- Where on the scale from darkness to light, from gloomy to radiant, is your life in Christ? What would help you to reflect his light more luminously?

- Who are three wise seekers to whom you look for advice and guidance today? What three gifts might you bring to honor Christ today?

- Imagine yourself as one of the Magi. What do you see? What do you hear? What emotions do you feel? How do you respond?

- In what way do these texts challenge you to be a global disciple of Christ and to extend your concern to all races and nations? What gifts have people of other cultures brought to you?

- Matthew's infancy narrative, in contrast to Luke's, is full of turmoil, danger, and suffering. It reminds us that the Word became flesh amid the harsh political and social realities of human history. How do these narratives prepare you for the adult ministry of Jesus and of his Church? How do they prepare you for your own ministry?

ORATIO

After allowing yourself to be disturbed and challenged by these Scripture texts, respond to God with the prayer that arises from your reflection. Begin with these words and allow them to spark your own words of prayer.

Lord of all the nations, you mark the path of my life with your shining light and you guide me on my journey to you. Give me the desire to kneel before you and present to you the gifts of my life.

Continue praying for openness to God's light and for the courage to follow wherever it leads you.

CONTEMPLATIO

As you move into silent contemplative prayer, choose a word, phrase, or image from the Scriptures to be your focus. Then just rest in God's presence, recalling and repeating the word, phrase, or image when you get distracted.

OPERATIO

People with odd dress, different-colored skin, and unintelligible language often put us on guard. Yet Epiphany celebrates these strangers as friends, companions on the journey, and coheirs with us to God's promises. What can you do this week to better appreciate the strangers among you? How can you recognize the gifts they bring, and how can you be grateful for the ways they help you to recognize Christ?

Chapter Seven

Lectio Divina for the Holy Family and the Baptism of the Lord: Years A, B, C

The Holy Family of Jesus, Mary, and Joseph: Year A

LECTIO

The feast of the Holy Family celebrates the fact that Jesus was born into a human family and shared in all the joys and challenges of family life. The Scriptures emphasize the family experiences that shape human existence.

Prepare yourself to read these sacred texts and to incorporate their values into your own life. Ask the Holy Spirit to help you continue to listen and respond to the sacra pagina during this Christmas season.

SIRACH 3:2-6, 12-14

God sets a father in honor over his children;
　a mother's authority he confirms over her sons.
Whoever honors his father atones for sins,
　and preserves himself from them.
When he prays, he is heard;
　he stores up riches who reveres his mother.
Whoever honors his father is gladdened by children,
　and, when he prays, is heard.
Whoever reveres his father will live a long life;
　he who obeys his father brings comfort to his mother.

My son, take care of your father when he is old;
grieve him not as long as he lives.
Even if his mind fail, be considerate of him;
revile him not all the days of his life;
kindness to a father will not be forgotten,
firmly planted against the debt of your sins
—a house raised in justice to you.

∧

The Book of Sirach reflects the wisdom gleaned from the author's personal experiences and his discernment of God's presence in everyday life. Although families live in different circumstances today, the values highlighted in this text are important for families in every era. Children must honor and respect their parents; they must comfort, revere, and take care of both their father and mother. Those who maintain these values will live a long life, receive God's forgiveness, and store up spiritual riches.

The text is addressed primarily to adult children. Men and women who honor their parents will be respected by their own children. Respect and care for elders are values that should be instilled in everyone, beginning in childhood. If this duty to honor the elders is not instilled in the early years, it is very difficult to develop later. Elders should be honored because they are the repositories of wisdom gleaned from life. Their hard work has earned the benefits enjoyed by the next generation. But no matter the age of parents or children, their love and respect are enduring and mutual.

Today people are living longer than ever before, in large part because of new medicines and better medical care. Many middle-aged adults face a double set of often burdensome responsibilities:

to both younger children and aging parents. Elderly parents are often faced with the loss of their independence and with the need to make major life changes so that they can live closer to their children. They may be grieving, fearful, or in chronic pain. We must treat our parents gently, patiently, and compassionately, even if they become irritable or difficult.

Of course, we need to rely on the grace of Christ to help us in honoring our parents. The Holy Family of Jesus, Mary, and Joseph can guide and inspire us, as they faced their own set of hardships. Listen with the ear of your heart to their challenges as narrated in Matthew's Gospel.

MATTHEW 2:13-15, 19-23

When the magi had departed, behold, the angel of the Lord appeared to Joseph in a dream and said, "Rise, take the child and his mother, flee to Egypt, and stay there until I tell you. Herod is going to search for the child to destroy him." Joseph rose and took the child and his mother by night and departed for Egypt. He stayed there until the death of Herod, that what the Lord had said through the prophet might be fulfilled,

Out of Egypt I called my son.

When Herod had died, behold, the angel of the Lord appeared in a dream to Joseph in Egypt and said, "Rise, take the child and his mother and go to the land of Israel, for those who sought the child's life are dead." He rose, took the child and his mother, and went to the land of Israel. But when he heard that Archelaus was ruling over Judea in place of his father Herod, he was afraid to go back there. And because he had been warned in a dream, he departed for the region of Galilee. He went and dwelt in a town called Nazareth, so that what had been spoken through the prophets might be fulfilled,

He shall be called a Nazorean.

Just as elders are the treasury of the past, so children are the hope of the future. The Gospel presents Joseph and Mary as models for parents of all ages. Their concern was for the security and welfare of their child. They put aside their own plans in order to secure protection and safety for the child entrusted to them by God.

Guided by God through his dreams, Joseph is instructed to flee with Mary and the child to Egypt because of Herod's intent to kill the infant Jesus. We can only imagine Mary and Joseph's fear as they stole away under the cover of darkness into the unknown. The Gospel does not recount details of their treacherous desert crossing, the dangers they faced, or the hardships they must have endured. We don't know the details of what happened when they arrived in that strange place and had to navigate an unfamiliar language and culture. We don't know how they managed their emotions, how they supported one another, or who helped them along the way. We only know that after a time had passed, they departed from Egypt and traveled to Nazareth.

What we do know is that the Holy Family faced many of the same types of hardship and distress that families face today. They were displaced people, fleeing from a brutal ruler in their own country, like so many exiles and refugee families of our times. A holy family is certainly not one secure from threatening dangers. The family of Jesus experienced the adversity and struggles that families face in every period of time.

The quotation from Hosea 11:1, "Out of Egypt I called my son" (Matthew 2:15), recalls Israel's exodus while presenting the journey of Jesus' family to return to Israel. The context of the prophetic passage offers a tender parental view of God for all those who trust in his providence: "When Israel was a child I loved him. / . . . It was I who taught Ephraim to walk, / who took them in my arms; / . . . I drew them with human cords, with bands of love; / I fostered them like those / who raise an infant to their cheeks; / I bent down to feed them" (Hosea 11:1, 3-4). This God who loves his people tenderly and affectionately is the Father of Jesus, who cared for him in his infancy through the parenting of Joseph and Mary. This divine parent is the model and guide for all parents who share in his creating, caring, saving love for their children.

MEDITATIO

Now that you have listened to the texts for this feast, allow the Scriptures to interact with your own experiences of family. Consider what personal messages and challenges these texts are offering to you.

- How do you understand God's instruction to honor your father and mother? What are the personal challenges this instruction offers to you?

- What aspects of family life are most enriching for you? What aspects are most challenging? What family values do you try to hand on to the next generation?

- In what ways does the love of a parent reflect the love of God? In what ways do your parenting instincts remind you of God's love?

- What are some of the struggles of immigrants and refugees? Why does God exhort his people to care for migrants and people in exile (see, for example, Exodus 23:9)?

- The Holy Family was a real family that faced real trials and crises. What can you learn from Joseph and Mary about parenting and the care of children? What makes a family holy?

ORATIO

In response to your listening and meditation, pray to God who loves you tenderly as a parent.

Compassionate Father, you guided and protected your children in their exodus from Egypt, bringing them home to their own land. Safeguard me and lead me to the places where I can best experience your presence and serve you.

Continue praying to the God who knows you intimately and provides for your needs.

CONTEMPLATIO

Place yourself in the affectionate embrace of God who loves you unconditionally. Let God's loving care transform your heart to trust in him unreservedly.

OPERATIO

Consider the needs of families who are immigrants, exiles, or refugees. Choose something you could do this week to support them with your time, talent, or treasure.

The Holy Family of Jesus, Mary, and Joseph: Year B

LECTIO

⋏

This feast celebrates the fact that God's revelation occurs in the context of human families. God begins a new action in the world as the families of Abraham and Sarah and Joseph and Mary faithfully trust in God's promises.

Call upon the renewing Spirit of God as you prepare to read the inspired Scriptures. Open yourself to whatever new insight or encouragement God wishes to offer you.

GENESIS 15:1-6; 21:1-3

The word of the LORD came to Abram in a vision, saying:
"Fear not, Abram!
I am your shield;
I will make your reward very great."
But Abram said, "O Lord GOD, what good will your gifts be, if I keep on being childless and have as my heir the steward of my house, Eliezer?" Abram continued, "See, you have given me no offspring, and so one of my servants will be my heir." Then the word of the LORD came to him: "No, that one shall not be your heir; your own issue shall be your heir." The Lord took Abram outside and said, "Look up at the sky and count the stars, if you can. Just so," he added, "shall

159

your descendants be." Abram put his faith in the LORD, who credited it to him as an act of righteousness.

The LORD took note of Sarah as he had said he would; he did for her as he had promised. Sarah became pregnant and bore Abraham a son in his old age, at the set time that God had stated. Abraham gave the name Isaac to this son of his whom Sarah bore him.

 ⅄

"Fear not," God calls to Abram (Genesis 15:1). Faith like that of Abram grows stronger over time, as fears are faced and overcome. God wants Abram to trust in the divine promise of an heir. After many years of waiting, God promises him a great reward. But Abram's pent-up frustrations burst forth in doubt and disappointment: "O Lord GOD, what good will your gifts be, if I keep on being childless?" (15:2). No material reward could ever equal the blessing of having a child.

Abram seems almost resigned to the fallback measure offered to childless couples. The barren couple would adopt a slave to care for them in their old age and assure a proper burial, and after their death, the adopted servant would become their principal heir. But God assures Abram with these promises: Not only will he have a child as an heir, but his offspring will be innumerable. To impress on Abram the enormity of this gift, God invites him to contemplate the star-studded night sky: "Just so shall your descendants be" (Genesis 15:5). Abram would have multitudes of offspring by natural birth, complemented by countless children joined to his lineage by faith.

Abram (renamed Abraham) puts his faith in God, placing his full trust in God's promises even when that trust seems unwarranted. And finally, God keeps his word: the brief narrative of Isaac's birth shows that God's promise has indeed come to fruition. The child's birth is the resolution of all the anxious waiting, worries, and doubts. The text shows how the lives of Abraham and Sarah are portraits of faithfulness and how they have become models of faith for us all.

Like Abraham and Sarah, Joseph and Mary trusted in God and expressed their faith by fulfilling the prescriptions of the covenant. Prepare to read the Gospel, expecting to hear God's voice anew and to be challenged by the faith of our ancestors.

LUKE 2:22-40

When the days were completed for their purification according to the law of Moses, they took him up to Jerusalem to present him to the Lord, just as it is written in the law of the Lord, *Every male that opens the womb shall be consecrated to the Lord,* and to offer the sacrifice of *a pair of turtledoves or two young pigeons,* in accordance with the dictate in the law of the Lord.

Now there was a man in Jerusalem whose name was Simeon. This man was righteous and devout, awaiting the consolation of Israel, and the Holy Spirit was upon him. It had been revealed to him by the Holy Spirit that he should not see death before he had seen the Christ of the Lord. He came in the Spirit into the temple; and when the parents brought in the child Jesus to perform the custom of the law in regard to him, he took him into his arms and blessed God, saying:

> "Now, Master, you may let your servant go
>   in peace, according to your word,
> for my eyes have seen your salvation,
>   which you prepared in sight of all the peoples,
> a light for revelation to the Gentiles,
>   and glory for your people Israel."

The child's father and mother were amazed at what was said about him; and Simeon blessed them and said to Mary his mother, "Behold, this child is destined for the fall and rise of many in Israel, and to be a sign that will be contradicted—and you yourself a sword will pierce—so that the thoughts of many hearts may be revealed." There was also a prophetess, Anna, the daughter of Phanuel, of the tribe of Asher. She was advanced in years, having lived seven years with her husband after her marriage, and then as a widow until she was eighty-four. She never left the temple, but worshiped night and day with fasting and prayer. And coming forward at that very time, she gave thanks to God and spoke about the child to all who were awaiting the redemption of Jerusalem.

When they had fulfilled all the prescriptions of the law of the Lord, they returned to Galilee, to their own town of Nazareth. The child grew and became strong, filled with wisdom; and the favor of God was upon him.

ㅅ

This continuation of Luke's infancy account demonstrates that the life of Jesus was rooted in the worship and institutions of ancient Israel. The observances of the Holy Family included the precepts of the covenant regarding the circumcision of the child, the purification of Mary after childbirth, and the presentation of the firstborn. This scene demonstrates how the covenant, the Temple, and the spirit of prophecy all form the context for God's new revelation.

The elderly Simeon and Anna represent the people of Israel who have waited for the fulfillment of God's promises to send the Messiah and restore his people. They are devout and righteous, at home in the Temple, moved by God's Spirit, and longing for the coming of God's salvation. They demonstrate that hope is rooted in memory and that God's new work is the fulfillment of old promises.

After Simeon proclaims a message of light, joy, and hope about Jesus, which brings amazement to Joseph and Mary, he then casts a dark shadow in a prophecy specifically addressed to Mary. The fulfillment of God's promises will be accomplished only at great cost. Her child will be "a sign that will be contradicted" (Luke 2:34), as he will be spurned and rejected by many. And Mary herself "a sword will pierce" (2:35), Simeon tells her, expressing the heartrending pain she will experience by her intimate association with Jesus, both as his mother and as his first disciple. Already the shadow of the cross begins to fall over the joyful scenes of the Messiah's birth.

The eighty-four-year-old Anna has experienced three stages of family life: as a single woman, as a married woman for seven years, and as a widow for the many years that followed. Her constant prayer and fasting have given her insights into the mystery of the child before her and what God has in store for her people through him. Her longing and hope are over, and she can now move off-stage as the new era of salvation begins in the ministry of Jesus.

MEDITATIO

- When do you need to hear the words "Fear not" (Genesis 15:1) in the context of family life? Why are doubts and fears a necessary part of growing in faith? How has your faith developed through times of fear and doubt?

- Why might God delay the fulfillment of his promises to us? When have you had to wait for God to act? Have you ever seen advantages in relying on God's timetable instead of your own?

- When have you found it most difficult to trust in God? In what way does your confidence in God give hope to your life? Why is patient expectation the necessary stance of every believer?

- How might Mary have felt when Simeon addressed the prophecy of the piercing sword to her? In what ways was this prophecy fulfilled through her years as the mother of Jesus?

- Why does this Gospel message of Simeon, Anna, Joseph, and Mary include both light and shadow? What does it mean to say that the cross has cast its shadow over the scenes of Jesus' infancy?

ORATIO

Respond to God's word with your own words of prayer. Include the ideas, images, and vocabulary of Scripture to enrich the content of your prayer. Use this prayer for a starter:

Lord God, I am grateful for the unearned gifts you have given me. Give me the gift of faith so that I may trust in you completely, the gift of hope that I may look to the future with confidence, and the gift of love that I may savor your gracious presence.

Continue to pray as your heart directs you.

CONTEMPLATIO

Abraham, Sarah, Simeon, and Anna waited many years to see the fulfillment of God's promises. Spend some moments resting in God's embrace, placing your life in God's hands and relying on him completely.

OPERATIO

In the context of their families, each of the figures in these Scriptures trusted in God completely. How would your life be different if you trusted in God completely? What can you do to begin living that kind of life today?

The Holy Family of Jesus, Mary, and Joseph: Year C

LECTIO

⋏

The Scripture readings for the feast of the Holy Family remind us that being family is an intimate involvement with God—more challenging than we expect and more rewarding than we could ever hope for. Ask the Holy Spirit to help you listen and respond to the sacra pagina as you reflect on these texts.

When you have quieted your external and internal distractions, dedicate this time for sacred conversation with God.

1 SAMUEL 1:20-22, 24-28

In those days Hannah conceived, and at the end of her term bore a son whom she called Samuel, since she had asked the LORD for him. The next time her husband Elkanah was going up with the rest of his household to offer the customary sacrifice to the LORD and to fulfill his vows, Hannah did not go, explaining to her husband, "Once the child is weaned, I will take him to appear before the LORD and to remain there forever; I will offer him as a perpetual nazirite."

Once Samuel was weaned, Hannah brought him up with her, along with a three-year-old bull, an ephah of flour, and a skin of wine, and presented him at the temple of the LORD in Shiloh. After the boy's father had sacrificed the young bull,

Hannah, his mother, approached Eli and said: "Pardon, my lord! As you live, my lord, I am the woman who stood near you here, praying to the LORD. I prayed for this child, and the LORD granted my request. Now I, in turn, give him to the LORD; as long as he lives, he shall be dedicated to the LORD." Hannah left Samuel there.

人

Elkanah and Hannah regularly went to worship God at the temple in Shiloh, where the ark of the covenant was then housed. During one of their pilgrimages, Hannah had poured out her grief over her barrenness and asked for the gift of a son, promising God that she would dedicate her son to God if he answered her prayer. When she explained her situation to Eli the priest, he blessed her and she left in peace.

Hannah then conceived and gave birth to a son, whom she named Samuel. After he is weaned, she takes her son to the temple along with a generous sacrifice, and she offers him to God. She leaves him there in the service of the temple.

As Samuel matures, he will be instrumental in the transition of God's people from a tribal confederacy to a unified monarchy under King David. Hannah's asking for a son and God's granting her request foreshadow the way the people will ask for a king and God will grant their request.

Similarly, the journey of Elkanah and Hannah to the temple at Shiloh foreshadows the pilgrimage of Joseph and Mary to the Temple in Jerusalem. As Elkanah and Hannah leave their child at "the temple of the LORD" (1 Samuel 1:24) to serve God there, Joseph and Mary discover that their son must also be in his Father's house. As Samuel brought God's people to the next stage of God's plan for them, the Son of David and Son of Mary will bring God's people to the final stage of their saving history.

Luke 2:41-52

Each year Jesus' parents went to Jerusalem for the feast of Passover, and when he was twelve years old, they went up according to festival custom. After they had completed its days, as they were returning, the boy Jesus remained behind in Jerusalem, but his parents did not know it. Thinking that he was in the caravan, they journeyed for a day and looked for him among their relatives and acquaintances, but not finding him, they returned to Jerusalem to look for him. After three days they found him in the temple, sitting in the midst of the teachers, listening to them and asking them questions, and all who heard him were astounded at his understanding and his answers. When his parents saw him, they were astonished, and his mother said to him, "Son, why have you done this to us? Your father and I have been looking for you with great anxiety." And he said to them, "Why were you looking for me? Did you not know that I must be in my Father's house?" But they did not understand what he said to them. He went down with them and came to Nazareth, and was obedient to them; and his mother kept all these things in her heart. And Jesus advanced in wisdom and age and favor before God and man.

Joseph and Mary regularly go to worship God at the Temple of God in Jerusalem. As they are returning home from one of their pilgrimages for the feast of Passover, they discover that Jesus is not in the caravan with their relatives and friends. They return to Jerusalem, and after three days of anxiously searching for him, they find him in the Temple, sitting in the midst of the teachers.

Jesus confronts his parents with words that would provide little consolation for any parent: "Why were you looking for me? Did you not know that I must be in my Father's house?" (Luke 2:49). Jesus' response makes it clear that his life involves obedience to more than earthly parents. Although Mary has just referred to Joseph as Jesus' father, Jesus uses the word "Father" to refer to the God of Israel.

Yet doing the will of his heavenly Father entails obedience to Mary and Joseph: "He went down with them and came to Nazareth, and was obedient to them" (Luke 2:51). Mary and Joseph have taught Jesus how to recognize the call of God and how to be obedient to it. In their home in Nazareth, he will continue to grow "in wisdom and age and favor" (2:52) and in his ability to discern the ways of obedience to God. Through his earthly parents, Jesus will come to understand how precious and beloved he is as God's chosen one.

MEDITATIO

Now seek to assimilate these sacred texts in all their depth so that you can respond to them throughout your life as a member of God's family.

- Why might God have waited so long before giving Hannah a son? How might Hannah have felt when she brought her son to the temple to offer him to God?

- Have you ever been separated from your parents or from your child? What was this experience of loss like for you?

- The narrative describing the finding of Jesus by Joseph and Mary in the Temple of Jerusalem serves as a transition in Luke's Gospel between Jesus' infancy and his adult ministry. What does the story tell you about Jesus and his early adolescence?

- What does this episode teach you about balancing the everyday responsibilities of family life with the attraction to the service of God and worship? How did the Holy Family integrate their family life and their life under God's covenant?

- What did Jesus learn from Mary and Joseph? What can you learn from the Holy Family about the joys, challenges, struggles, and blessings of family life?

ORATIO

ᘡ

Pray for the grace to treasure in your heart, as Mary did, the ways of God that we do not immediately understand.

You, O Lord, are my rock and my fortress; for your name's sake you will lead and guide me. You will free me from the snare they set for me, for you are my refuge. Into your hands I commend my spirit; you will redeem me, O Lord, O faithful God.

Continue to pray in your own words, seeking to imitate Jesus' complete trust in the Father.

CONTEMPLATIO

ᘡ

The Gospel says that Mary "kept all these things in her heart" (Luke 2:51). Spend some moments in silence uniting your heart with hers. Slowly repeat Mary's response to God at her Annunciation: "May it be done to me according to your word" (1:38).

OPERATIO

ᘡ

The desire of the Holy Family to live in obedience to God's will is an inspiration to all families. What are some ways in which you might better respond to God's calling among your family? Include some special kindness for a member of your family among your New Year's resolutions.

The Baptism of the Lord: Year A

LECTIO

ʌ

This Sunday serves as both the end of the Christmas season and the First Sunday of Ordinary Time. As the beginning of Jesus' adult ministry, these Scripture readings do not let us forget the joy of the Incarnation; they remind us of our own need to be reborn every day in the Spirit of Jesus.

Read these texts aloud, vocalizing the words of the text so that you not only read with your eyes but speak with your lips and hear with your ears. Listen deeply to God's word in your heart.

Isaiah 42:1-4, 6-7

Thus says the LORD:

Here is my servant whom I uphold,
  my chosen one with whom I am pleased,
upon whom I have put my spirit;
  he shall bring forth justice to the nations,
not crying out, not shouting,
  not making his voice heard in the street.
A bruised reed he shall not break,
  and a smoldering wick he shall not quench,

until he establishes justice on the earth;
    the coastlands will wait for his teaching.

I, the LORD, have called you for the victory of justice,
    I have grasped you by the hand;
I formed you, and set you
    as a covenant of the people,
    a light for the nations,
to open the eyes of the blind,
    to bring out prisoners from confinement,
    and from the dungeon, those who live in darkness.

This text from the prophet Isaiah introduces God's "servant," his "chosen one" (Isaiah 42:1), upon whom God has placed his divine spirit. Whether this servant was originally an ideal prophet, an ideal king, or the personification of ideal Israel, Jesus understood his own messianic ministry as the fulfillment of Isaiah's Servant passages. He is that Servant, empowered by God to carry out the divine mission for the sake of the whole earth.

The purpose for which God calls the Servant is "the victory of justice" (Isaiah 42:6). Three times in these verses, God's Servant is called to establish justice among the nations (42:1, 4, 6). But he will accomplish this justice, not through conflict and the strength of arms, but with patient gentleness. He will support bent reeds rather than trampling upon them; he will fan flickering flames rather than dousing them. His manner of witness stands in stark contrast to the ways of the nations and their leaders. The reign of justice seems to be promoted through the renunciation of force and with particular sensitivity to the weak and vulnerable.

The text highlights the universal dimension of the Servant's mission. As "a covenant of the people, a light for the nations" (Isaiah 42:6), the Servant is the instrument whereby all people are drawn into Israel's covenant with God and through which all nations will come to share in the light of God. For Isaiah, the coming of this Servant was a hope that he never saw realized. Yet many centuries later, Jesus searched these prophecies of Isaiah in trying to discern the implications of his own mission. At his baptism, Jesus is empowered by God to carry out the Servant's mission. Read Matthew's account of Jesus' baptism with Isaiah's vision in mind.

MATTHEW 3:13-17

Jesus came from Galilee to John at the Jordan to be baptized by him. John tried to prevent him, saying, "I need to be baptized by you, and yet you are coming to me?" Jesus said to him in reply, "Allow it now, for thus it is fitting for us to fulfill all righteousness." Then he allowed him. After Jesus was baptized, he came up from the water and behold, the heavens were opened for him, and he saw the Spirit of God descending like a dove and coming upon him. And a voice came from the heavens, saying, "This is my beloved Son, with whom I am well pleased."

The baptism of Jesus by John the Baptist inaugurates his public ministry. From Matthew's infancy narrative, we have already learned that Jesus is the Messiah, Son of God, Son of David, and King of the Jews. From Matthew's description of John the Baptist, the prophet of Advent, we know that John was preparing the way of the Lord and looking forward to the "mightier" one (Luke 3:16) coming after him. At last the adult Jesus steps onto the public stage and comes to John at the Jordan River to seek his baptism.

Like the Servant in Isaiah, Jesus is God's chosen one with whom God is well pleased. He is the one upon whom God has put his Spirit, opening a new hope-filled era in the history of God's saving action. The gentle descent of the Spirit like a dove evokes peaceful-ness and the possibilities for a new beginning, like the dove that brought Noah the signs of hope for new life. Just as the mission of the Servant is centered on justice, so Jesus intends "to fulfill all righteousness" (Matthew 3:15). "Righteousness" or "justice" expresses God's fidelity and right relationship with Israel as well as the proper human response to God and others. Jesus brings to completion the justice that God desired and ordained for all people and shows us how to bring this justice to the world. God's most radical way of bringing everyone into right relationship with him is through Jesus' Incarnation and baptism and his obedience to all that God desires.

The identity and mission of Jesus, already revealed in the nar-ratives of his conception and birth, are here manifested in a new epiphany on the banks of the Jordan River. Jesus sees the Spirit of God descending on him like a dove, and then all the onlookers hear the voice from the heavens saying, "This is my beloved Son, with whom I am well pleased" (Matthew 3:17). We who follow Jesus, who are baptized into him, have the same assurance. We are beloved sons and daughters of God, not because of our own efforts or merits now or in the future, but because of God's gift of union with his own Son. Through him a new communication and a new relationship is opened between God and the people of the earth.

MEDITATIO

Spend some time reflecting on the biblical passages you have read, allowing them to interact with your own world of memories, questions, ideas, and concerns, until you are aware of the personal messages the texts offer to you.

- What terms in Isaiah's prophecy express the Servant's relationship to God? His character? His mission?

- In what ways does Jesus fulfill Isaiah's description of God's Servant? What does this tell you about his character and mission?

- Jesus insisted on being baptized by John even though he was sinless. What does this tell you about Jesus and his solidarity with humanity?

- Christian baptism is both adoption into the very life of God and a mission to proclaim justice, to be a light for the nations, to open the eyes of the blind, and to free prisoners from their dungeons (Isaiah 42:6-7). In what ways might you be called to live out your baptism more fully?

- In what sense is the feast of the Baptism of Jesus both the end of the Christmas season and the beginning of Ordinary Time? What do you want to take from your lectio divina during these weeks into the "ordinary time" of your daily life?

ORATIO

∧

After listening and reflecting on the word of God, respond to that word with heartfelt and embodied prayer. Let this prayer be an incentive to continue with your own:

Lord God, you have formed your Servant, grasped him by the hand, and called him to establish justice on the earth. Stir up the grace of my own baptism. Send your Spirit upon me, guide me with your hand, give me a passion for justice, and make me generous in your service.

Continue to pray in whatever words your heart directs.

CONTEMPLATIO

∧

As followers of Jesus, we are people on whom the waters of baptism are never dry. Ask God's Spirit to descend upon you and renew the grace of baptism within you. Realize that your life is united in the Father, the Son, and the Holy Spirit. Spend some quiet moments in union with the source of the divine life within you.

OPERATIO

Your own baptism is a commission to share in the mission of God's Servant, to "bring forth justice to the nations" (Isaiah 42:1). Consider ways in which you may be a public witness to the teachings of Jesus, and choose one way in which you can witness to God's justice for the world.

The Baptism of the Lord: Year B

LECTIO

ᴧ

The feast of the Baptism of the Lord is a bridge between the Christmas season and Ordinary Time. At this threshold leading to Christ's adult ministry, John the Baptist reveals Jesus, continuing the revelation of Jesus to shepherds and Magi celebrated at Christmas and Epiphany.

Call upon the same Holy Spirit who inspired the sacred writers to fill your heart and kindle in you the fire of divine love. When you are ready, listen carefully to the words of these inspired texts.

ISAIAH 55:1-11

Thus says the LORD:

All you who are thirsty,
    come to the water!
You who have no money,
    come, receive grain and eat;
come, without paying and without cost,
    drink wine and milk!
Why spend your money for what is not bread,
    your wages for what fails to satisfy?
Heed me, and you shall eat well,

you shall delight in rich fare.
Come to me heedfully,
    listen, that you may have life.
I will renew with you the everlasting covenant,
    the benefits assured to David.
As I made him a witness to the peoples,
    a leader and commander of nations,
so shall you summon a nation you knew not,
    and nations that knew you not shall run to you,
because of the LORD, your God,
    the Holy One of Israel, who has glorified you.

Seek the LORD while he may be found,
    call him while he is near.
Let the scoundrel forsake his way,
    and the wicked man his thoughts;
let him turn to the LORD for mercy;
    to our God, who is generous in forgiving.
For my thoughts are not your thoughts,
    nor are your ways my ways, says the LORD.
As high as the heavens are above the earth
    so high are my ways above your ways
    and my thoughts above your thoughts.

For just as from the heavens
    the rain and snow come down
and do not return there
    till they have watered the earth,
    making it fertile and fruitful,

giving seed to the one who sows
   and bread to the one who eats,
so shall my word be
   that goes forth from my mouth;
my word shall not return to me void,
   but shall do my will,
   achieving the end for which I sent it.

Through the prophet Isaiah, God invites all people to "come to the water" (Isaiah 55:1), to that precious gift without which we cannot live. The water is God's salvation, the spring of deliverance, the river of redemption, a gift that is freely offered and can be freely refused. The offer of flowing water is extended to a feast of food and drink, a banquet of rich fare, to which all are invited regardless of wealth or social position. The only requirement is simply hunger and thirst.

To the exiles in Babylon, God announces that their salvation comes not just from a physical return to Jerusalem but from a heartfelt return to him. "Come to me heedfully, listen, that you may have life" (Isaiah 55:3). God is renewing the everlasting covenant with his people. However, the people of the covenant will now summon other nations, and other peoples will run to the God who invites all to the banquet of salvation.

God's loving command, directed to those whose hearts have not yet returned to God, is this one: "Seek the LORD" (Isaiah 55:6). The command is not punitive; instead, it is rich in mercy and filled with divine compassion. The blessings of God's covenant await his people like an open door. Why, then, would some refuse to turn to God? Does the fault lie with God? Human logic might say yes, for if God possesses sufficient power and care for his people, Jerusalem would not have been destroyed and the people would not be in exile. However, such limited logic is incapable of grasping the truth.

Those who fail to grasp in faith the truth proclaimed by God's prophet will continue to stumble in the darkness of exile. For God says, "My thoughts are not your thoughts, nor are your ways my ways" (Isaiah 55:8). Unless human beings turn aside from their smug pride and rationalizing defenses and stand in humble awe before the Lord, they cannot receive God's gracious offer. They will not understand that the water of salvation and the banquet of life are free for those who confess the inadequacy of their own solutions and desire God's thoughts and God's ways.

Isaiah urges us to have confidence in God's word. Just as God sends the rain and snow to water the earth and make it fertile and fruitful, God sends his word to accomplish his will in us. Faithfully God has delivered his word to all the people of the earth. When we heed God's word and receive it in faith, the fruit of salvation springs up within us.

The word of God in Isaiah prepares us for God's word proclaimed in the Gospel. The invitation to the water of salvation becomes the Sacrament of Baptism. The summons to the banquet of life becomes the Sacrament of the Eucharist. Through his word, God invites us to share deeply in the life of his beloved Son.

MARK 1:7-11

This is what John the Baptist proclaimed: "One mightier than I is coming after me. I am not worthy to stoop and loosen the thongs of his sandals. I have baptized you with water; he will baptize you with the Holy Spirit."

It happened in those days that Jesus came from Nazareth of Galilee and was baptized in the Jordan by John. On coming up out of the water he saw the heavens being torn open and the Spirit, like a dove, descending upon him. And a voice came from the heavens, "You are my beloved Son; with you I am well pleased."

As Isaiah the prophet summoned God's exiled people to the waters of salvation, John the Baptist calls them to the Jordan River. His baptism is a ritual of repentance, but the mightier One coming after him will baptize with the Holy Spirit. Again God's merciful forgiveness awaits God's people like an open door.

In his first public manifestation, Jesus arrives from the village of Nazareth. Although he is without sin, he places himself in total solidarity with the crowd and with sinful humanity. He takes on the guilt of all people in allowing himself to be lowered into the water. As he rises from the water, the heavens are "torn open" (Mark 1:10), never to be shut again, inaugurating a new relationship between God and the earth. Through God's gracious gash in the universe, God's Spirit descends upon Jesus, empowering Jesus as his Messiah and acknowledging Jesus as his beloved Son.

The baptism of John prepared God's people for the coming of Jesus the Messiah. But the baptism that Jesus brought through the Holy Spirit initiates believers into the new age of God's grace. This exchange between the Father, Son, and Holy Spirit demonstrates the relationship to which God calls all people. Through baptism into the Spirit-filled and beloved Son, we become beloved sons and daughters of God and are commissioned to serve God's kingdom in his name.

MEDITATIO

Both Isaiah and John the Baptist speak the word of God and point to the coming of Christ. Let their message instill God's fertile and fruitful word within you.

- On what things have you spent your money and your labor that failed to satisfy and were ultimately unfulfilling? What message does Isaiah speak to this unprofitable use of your life?

- In what ways do flowing water and a richly satisfying banquet express the new life you have received through faith in Jesus Christ? How can you invite another person to experience this salvation?

- What is Isaiah saying about the power of God's word by comparing it to the rain and snow? In what ways does this give you confidence as you listen to the Scriptures and reflect on them in faith?

- When have you experienced a deep sense of call and mission? Who are those people who have helped you in your journey of faith and deeper entry into the mystery of Jesus Christ?

- Jesus' death and resurrection were foreshadowed as he descended into the waters of John's baptism, taking with him the guilt of humanity, and rose from the waters to receive the descending Spirit. Do you view your baptism as a descent and ascent into new life in Christ? Why or why not?

ORATIO

God's prophets, Isaiah and John the Baptist, invite you to experience the salvation and life that come from knowing and loving Jesus Christ. Ask God for the gift of trusting confidence in his grace. Let these words be your prayer starter:

Father, through Jesus your beloved Son, you have made us all your daughters and sons. Help me accept my identity as your beloved child through the anointing of your Holy Spirit. As I continue to listen with confidence to your word, guide me in the mission you have entrusted to me.

Continue to pray whatever words well up from the depths of your heart.

CONTEMPLATIO

Remain in restful quiet, experiencing the joyful invitation offered by these Scriptures. Open yourself to receive whatever spiritual gifts God desires to give you during these moments as you place your trust in the grace of Jesus Christ.

OPERATIO

You have been offered the gift of salvation through Jesus Christ and have been baptized into his life. Consider the ways in which you could help prepare others for this transforming encounter. Choose one way to invite another to "seek the LORD" (Isaiah 55:6) this week.

The Baptism of the Lord: Year C

LECTIO

⋏

While in some ways this feast of the Baptism of the Lord may be an end, it is also a beginning. It is the end of the Christmas season and the beginning of Ordinary Time in the Church's liturgical calendar. It is also the end of this season of lectio divina and the beginning of your incorporating these practices more deeply into your everyday life.

When you are ready, begin reading these familiar texts as if for the first time, trying to let go of your own presumptions so that you can listen to God speaking to you anew.

ISAIAH 40:1-5, 9-11

Comfort, give comfort to my people,
  says your God.
Speak to the heart of Jerusalem, and proclaim to her
    that her service has ended,
    that her guilt is expiated,
That she has received from the hand of the LORD
    double for all her sins.

    A voice proclaims:
In the wilderness prepare the way of the LORD!

Make straight in the wasteland a highway for our God!
Every valley shall be lifted up,
   every mountain and hill made low;
The rugged land shall be a plain,
   the rough country, a broad valley.
Then the glory of the Lord shall be revealed,
   and all flesh shall see it together;
   for the mouth of the Lord has spoken.

Go up onto a high mountain,
   Zion, herald of good news!
Cry out at the top of your voice,
   Jerusalem, herald of good news!
Cry out, do not fear!
   Say to the cities of Judah:
   Here is your God!
Here comes with power
   the Lord God,
   who rules by his strong arm;
Here is his reward with him,
   his recompense before him.
Like a shepherd he feeds his flock;
   in his arms he gathers the lambs,
Carrying them in his bosom,
   leading the ewes with care.

These words of the prophet were first proclaimed to God's people who had been taken into exile by their Babylonian conquerors.

In the worst disaster of their history, they had been deported from their homeland while their beloved city and Temple had been destroyed. They had lost nearly everything that gave them identity, and it seemed as though God had abandoned them.

Into this utter desolation God speaks words of great consolation. God is instructing his emissaries to convey the message of comfort, pardon, and redemption to the broken community. The divine words "Comfort, give comfort top my people" (Isaiah 40:1) offer soothing reassurance, like a parent soothing a child after a bad dream. God assures his people that their time of exile, in which Israel had experienced so much loss and shame, has come to an end. Through Israel's repentance and God's forgiveness, peace has returned, and God will again answer the promises he had given through the intimate bond of Israel's covenant.

The ultimate purpose of God's coming to redeem his people is so that the glory of God will be revealed to all humanity. The "glory of the Lord" (Isaiah 40:5) is the manifestation of God's presence and saving power. This revelation to all people—"all flesh shall see it together" (40:5)—offers salvation to the whole world through the God of Israel.

Isaiah's prophecy proclaims the glad tidings that a new day has arisen for those held in the exile of Babylon. God is leading his people home again to Jerusalem. The "good news" (Isaiah 40:9) is something to shout and sing about. Indeed, the glory of the Lord is coming up over the mountain like the dawn of a new day. The climactic announcement is reached as Jerusalem/Zion is called to recognize God's imminent coming: "Here is your God!" (55:9). This coming of God to his people is elaborated through the two contrasting images that follow: God comes as the victorious warrior who rules with his strong arm and as the gentle shepherd who gathers the lambs in his arms.

Learning from Isaiah that God was doing something new for his people in every generation, the early Church looked to his prophecy as an announcement of the Messiah's coming. The Christmas season has announced his coming in the flesh; this feast of Christ's baptism announces his coming in ministry. Listen to Luke's account of how Jesus came to fulfill the expectations of God's people longing for salvation.

LUKE 3:15-16, 21-22

The people were filled with expectation, and all were asking in their hearts whether John might be the Christ. John answered them all, saying, "I am baptizing you with water, but one mightier than I is coming. I am not worthy to loosen the thongs of his sandals. He will baptize you with the Holy Spirit and fire."

After all the people had been baptized and Jesus also had been baptized and was praying, heaven was opened and the Holy Spirit descended upon him in bodily form like a dove. And a voice came from heaven, "You are my beloved Son; with you I am well pleased."

The preparation of God's people in the days of exile serves as a model for the preparatory repentance that was needed once again at the coming of the Messiah. All four Gospels begin the story of

Jesus' saving ministry with the witness of John the Baptist and his baptism of repentance. Isaiah's announcement of God's coming to save his people is recognized by the Gospel writers as completed in the coming of Jesus Christ.

Jesus' identity and his ministry are confirmed with his anointing by the Spirit at the time of his baptism and by the voice from heaven. This was the same voice that stilled the unruly waters of chaos at creation and created an ordered universe that would produce much life. Out of the waters of the Jordan River stepped an unpretentious man who would transform the world.

We, too, emerge from the waters at the time of our baptism, waters that have been transformed by God's word, and we are commissioned to continue the ministry that he has begun. As baptized people, we live in a world in which heaven has been opened and the divide between humanity and divinity has been dissolved. The Holy Spirit has descended on the Church and upon each of us, and the special place that Jesus holds in God's affection has been extended to us all.

MEDITATIO

Let these Scriptures touch your heart by reflecting on them in light of your own experiences of trust and hope.

- In the days of Isaiah, the coming of a king was announced by his herald, and the people would literally level the roads on which the king would travel. What does this metaphor tell you about preparing for the coming of the Messiah?

- Why were the tender words of Isaiah so comforting for God's people? Which words of Isaiah are most comforting for you?

- What obstacles need to be removed for you to experience the work of the Messiah in your life? What needs to be raised, lowered, straightened, or smoothed?

- God comes to his people both as a powerful ruler and as a gentle shepherd. When have you experienced God in each of these ways? Why do we need both images of God?

- Recall the grace of your own baptism and realize that grace is just as active as on the day of your new birth in Christ. What particular mission is God calling you to do as his baptized child?

ORATIO

It is God's grace at work within us that gives us a desire to pray. Respond to the word of God that you have heard by lifting up your voice to God and expressing the contents of your heart:

Tender and compassionate God, you have heard the cries of your people and have announced the comforting words of salvation. Rescue me from the bondage of sin, fill me with your Spirit, stir up the grace of baptism within me, and send me forth to proclaim the gospel to others.

Continue your prayer by giving thanks for the life you have been given in baptism.

CONTEMPLATIO

When the words of prayer are no longer necessary or helpful, move into a wordless silence in the divine presence. God comes both as a powerful ruler and as a gentle shepherd. Try to call forth whichever expression of God you need most today.

OPERATIO

Our Christian baptism calls us to be active disciples of Jesus in the world. The practice of lectio divina shows us how to listen and respond to God's word in a way that makes a difference in our lives. In what way might God be calling you to a more active discipleship through your experience of lectio divina during the Advent and Christmas seasons?

Calendar of
Sunday Lectionary Cycles

The lectionary cycle for the Sunday liturgical readings begins each year on the First Sunday of Advent and ends each year on the last Sunday of Ordinary Time, which is the Solemnity of Christ the King. Here are the cycles that will be used by the Church through 2023.

Advent 2012 to Christ the King 2013: Year C

Advent 2013 to Christ the King 2014: Year A

Advent 2014 to Christ the King 2015: Year B

Advent 2015 to Christ the King 2016: Year C

Advent 2016 to Christ the King 2017: Year A

Advent 2017 to Christ the King 2018: Year B

Advent 2018 to Christ the King 2019: Year C

Advent 2019 to Christ the King 2020: Year A

Advent 2020 to Christ the King 2021: Year B

Advent 2021 to Christ the King 2022: Year C

Advent 2022 to Christ the King 2023: Year A

Conversing with God Lectio Divina Series

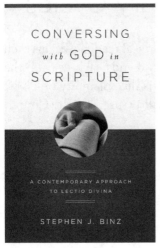

Conversing with God in
Scripture:
A Contemporary Approach
to Lectio Divina

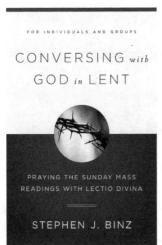

Conversing with God
in Lent:
Praying the Sunday Mass
Readings with Lectio Divina

From The Word Among Us Press

Conversing with God
in Advent and Christmas:
Praying the Sunday Mass
Readings with Lectio Divina

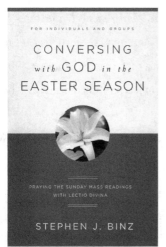

Conversing with God in the
Easter Season:
Praying the Sunday Mass
Readings with Lectio Divina

theWORD
among us ®
The *Spirit* of Catholic Living

This book was published by The Word Among Us. For nearly thirty years, The Word Among Us has been answering the call of the Second Vatican Council to help Catholic laypeople encounter Christ in the Scriptures—a call reiterated recently by Pope Benedict XVI and a Synod of Bishops.

The name of our company comes from the prologue to the Gospel of John and reflects the vision and purpose of all of our publications: to be an instrument of the Spirit, whose desire is to manifest Jesus' presence in and to the children of God. In this way, we hope to contribute to the Church's ongoing mission of proclaiming the gospel to the world and growing ever more deeply in our love for the Lord.

Our monthly devotional magazine, *The Word Among Us*, features meditations on the daily and Sunday Mass readings, and currently reaches more than one million Catholics in North America each year and another 500,000 Catholics in 100 countries. Our press division has published nearly 180 books and Bible studies over the past ten years.

To learn more about who we are and what we publish, log on to our Web site at **www.wau.org**. There you will find a variety of Catholic resources that will help you grow in your faith.

Embrace His Word, Listen to God . . .